DEAD BUT NOT BURIED

Aunt Gori,

Turn your adversity into opportunity!

DEAD BUT NOT BURIED

A MODERN DAY MIRACLE OF TRIUMPH OVER TRAGEDY

MARK L. FRANZMAN

ACW Press
Phoenix, Arizona 85013

Dead But Not Buried: A Modern Day Miracle of Triumph over Tragedy
Copyright ©2003 Mark L. Franzman
All rights reserved

Cover Design by Alpha Advertising
Interior design by Pine Hill Graphics

Packaged by ACW Press
5501 N. 7th Ave., #502
Phoenix, Arizona 85013
www.acwpress.com
The views expressed or implied in this work do not necessarily reflect those of ACW Press. Ultimate design, content, and editorial accuracy of this work is the responsibility of the author(s).

Library of Congress Cataloging-in-Publication Data
(Provided by Quality Books, Inc.)

Franzman, Mark L.
    Dead but not buried : a modern day miracle of triumph
over tragedy / Mark L. Franzman. -- 1st ed.
    p. cm.
    ISBN 1-892525-91-7

    1. Near death experiences--Religious aspects--
Christianity. 2. Franzman, Mark L. 3. Near death
experiences--Personal narratives. 4. Police--Florida--
Biography. I. Title.

BT833.F73 2002   236'.1
                          QBI33-653

Printed in the United States of America.

DEDICATION

For my mother, Betty, and my father, Fred:

You were always there for me from the beginning of this long journey to recovery. Every pain I felt you felt. I love you both as much as any son possibly can!

For my wife and best friend Linda, since the day we met at church you have been so supportive of me. You are such an encouragement and prayer warrior for me. God truly has blessed me with you!

For Alexandria, my step daughter whom I love dearly. You have made your mother and me very proud in the way you have developed into such a beautiful and godly young lady.

For Makayla, at the writing of this book we have yet to see you. Your mother and I love you very much and already consider you a part of this family. We are so anxious and excited about coming to China and adopting you, and then bringing you back with us to your new home in America. We are excited to see what wonderful things God has planned for your life.

For all the men and women in law enforcement, fire departments, medical facilities, and emergency medical services around this country, I salute you as America's heroes. Your endless dedication, professionalism, and sacrifices are greatly appreciated. You should be proud of the service you are in.

ONE

Growing Up

I grew up in the wonderful community of Fairfax, Virginia and led a normal life as a young boy. My father, Fred, was a retired colonel in the Marine Corps, and a school teacher at Robinson Secondary High School. My mother, Betty, was a homemaker and the best mother a son could ever hope of having. My sister Cheri was a lover of books and to this day she loves to read. I consider myself lucky to be raised in a loving and nurturing family.

As a boy I loved to play outdoors. One of my favorite games was a version of cowboys and Indians. I loved the action hero Zorro, so I would put on black pants and shirt, tie a cape around my neck, and place a mask over my eyes. The imaginary villains I conquered would not discover my identity. I carried a sword that had a hollow tip, so a piece of chalk could be attached at the end. This enabled me to leave my mark of "Z" after each and every victory over evil. There wasn't a tree (or side of a house) that was safe from my "Z" signature. I always wanted to play the good guy, never the villain. Even at a young age, I wanted to save the day.

As a child I had but one dream, and that was to be a police officer. When teachers asked, "What do you want to be when you grow up?" they recorded the students' responses on the back of their report cards. My mother saved all my report cards and my response was the same year after year: "I want to be a police officer!"

In the summer of 1976, my parents bought a motel on Clearwater Beach, Florida. My dad was retiring from teaching and wanted to move to Florida because we had fallen in love with the beach after many vacations in the area. My dad had mentioned to the owner of a particular motel where we had vacationed that he was interested in purchasing a motel on the beach. He later shocked my dad by telling him that the motel where we spent our summer vacations was going to be put up for sale! Sure enough, they worked it out and Dad bought the motel. I could hardly believe it. I was going to be moving to Florida, and if that weren't exciting enough, I was going to be living on the beach.

That next year I enrolled in Clearwater High School to complete my senior year. I had played on the football team in Virginia and now was trying out for the new team, the Clearwater High Tornadoes. I soon befriended a young man on the team named Mark Anderson. His father, I later learned, was the pastor of Calvary Baptist Church in downtown Clearwater. Soon I was attending church with him. My life was changed forever spiritually. After speaking with Mark about spiritual matters on our way to school every morning and attending a church revival at Calvary, I became a Christian by praying and inviting Christ into my heart. I joined the church and made many friends from the youth department. One of the first adults that I met at the church made a lasting impression on me, even to this day. Sam Raney was a large man with a strong Southern accent. What impressed me most about Sam was his warm and friendly personality, housed within such a big man. Sam was a captain for one of the local police departments. Before long Sam knew of my dream to become a police officer. I believe I reminded him of that dream every day!

When I joined the church basketball league, I discovered that one of the officials for the games was a police officer for the city of Clearwater. We became friends as well. I asked an annoying number of questions about police work after each and every basketball game. I soon found myself riding at nights, as an observer, as he patrolled the city streets. This confirmed in my heart that although my surroundings had changed drastically the past year, my childhood dream had not.

TWO

My Childhood
Dream Comes True

In 1979 I sent my resume to five or six agencies in the area. Sam Raney called me one afternoon and asked me if I was still interested in becoming a police officer. "It's still my dream, Sam," I told him. He asked me to meet with him the next morning at the Dunedin Police Department. That night a thousand things rushed through my mind. Was my childhood dream coming true? I tried not to think about it because I didn't want to be disappointed. Sam never mentioned that the department was hiring. He had only told me to come to the police station, take a look around and he would answer any questions I might have.

I asked him a thousand questions that morning. Sam had me sit in on a training session in one of the conference rooms. The room was full of uniformed officers; My heart ached to be in one of those uniforms and I couldn't imagine doing anything else as a career. After the training session was over, Sam told me to walk around and ask the employees and officers how they liked their jobs. Every officer I spoke with that morning said how great it was working for the department. I was sold. Sign me up!

Later that afternoon Sam called me to his office and asked me what I thought of the agency and employees. I told him speaking with the officers that day had only reinforced my feelings toward the profession. Sam then introduced me to the police chief who asked me a few questions and then asked me when I could go to work for the agency. I was in shock! I never thought I would be offered a job that day. I was only visiting with Sam to check out where he worked and to get a few questions answered. I couldn't contain my excitement. A childhood dream was coming true. I quickly answered, "I can start today!" Sam smiled, and the chief said, "How about next Monday?"

For months after the meeting with Captain Sam Raney, my feet never touched the ground. I excelled through the police academy, making excellent grades on my exams and qualifying as an expert with my weapon at the pistol range. I ate, slept, and drank law enforcement. I was so proud in putting on the police cadet uniform. It wasn't a handsome uniform like the officers on the street wore, but I was proud just the same. On graduation day we were instructed to wear our new police officer uniforms. This was the *real* thing! My dream was finally coming true! As I stood in front of the mirror in the dressing room at the academy, staring at myself in the official uniform that Dunedin officers have so proudly worn over the years, it hit me. My hard work had finally paid off. I was now *Officer* Mark Franzman.

As they called me to the platform during the graduation ceremony, my parents stood with Captain Sam Raney and the police chief. I recited the Police Officer's Oath and was sworn in as a police officer for the city of Dunedin. My mother and father pinned my badge on my starched and freshly pressed uniform shirt. My father was a man of few words and very seldom showed his emotions, but that evening I saw my dad beaming with pride and joy.

THREE

I'm an Officer

I grew up quickly once I hit the streets with my training officer. At age twenty-one, I learned how naïve I really was. I loved my new career so much that I would volunteer to work a second shift. I was single then so I had all the time and freedom I needed to put into my career. And I put a lot into it! Before I knew it I had almost three years of experience as a police officer under my belt. I was living out my childhood dream and loving it.

I also made a lot of friends at the police department. We had become like a close family. I remember moving furniture and boxes on many occasions on days off when fellow officers needed help moving.

When an officer was out for an extended time with an illness, several of us would go over to his house and cut his grass and pick up groceries for him each week. This bond among police officers develops due to the work we do. We look out for each other on the streets and would lay our lives down for each other as well as the citizens we are hired to protect.

America has seen the greatest example of this during the terrorist attack of September 11, 2001. Police officers, fire department personnel, and paramedics were all racing into the Twin Towers for one common purpose, to help the citizens in those burning and crumbling buildings. Never once did concerns for their own safety cause them to hesitate in their heroic actions. Those brave men and women in uniforms paid the ultimate price in trying to help total strangers. Professionals just like them have been doing that all over this country for decades.

FOUR

The Crash

Halloween, 1981. I was scheduled to work the evening shift, from 3:00 P.M. to 11:00 P.M. I felt this particular night was going to be different than any other night I had ever worked, but I couldn't explain the feelings. I knew deep down something was going to happen, so much so that I remember talking to an old high school buddy from Virginia before I left for work that evening. I told him in our phone conversation that I felt in my gut that something big was going to happen at work that night. I figured it would be a "Hot Call," such as a robbery, brawl, burglary-in-progress, or maybe a high-speed pursuit. Never would I have guessed that my life would change forever!

As I arrived at the police station that afternoon, I sensed tension at the read-off. (Read-off is when officers are told what to look for and what, if anything, happened the previous shift that could affect them during their shift). Historically, Halloween night is a busy night for police departments across the entire country. A lot of crazy things happen. Robberies increase, bar fights occur throughout the night, and drunk drivers are more prevalent due to all the parties. I still felt in my gut that something big was going to happen, but I wasn't about to share my feelings with any of the veteran officers on my shift that evening. I didn't want them to think I was crazy or worried.

I was assigned to work Zone 3, an eastern section of the city, comprised mostly of residential neighborhoods, with some bars, banks, small businesses, and shopping centers. That shift proved to be busy: I responded to several brawls, kids in costumes throwing eggs, loud parties, and an occasional domestic disturbance. I was scheduled to work until 11:00 P.M. but I had agreed earlier to help a fellow officer and friend by working the first half of his midnight shift.

At around 1:30 A.M., our communications division advised me and several other officers to respond to U.S. Highway 19, a large and congested highway that runs from south to north Florida. The dispatcher advised us there was a fatality crash being investigated by the Florida Highway Patrol. They needed our assistance in directing traffic around the wreck so they could complete their traffic homicide investigation. As I arrived on scene, the area was covered with debris from what was left of two burned and mangled vehicles. I was told that both drivers were drunk and one was killed upon impact. The other was fighting for his life at the emergency room. The troopers said the impact was so great that the cars exploded into one large ball of fire. Pieces from those vehicles went flying everywhere.

My assignment at the scene was to direct northbound traffic around the wreckage so troopers could concentrate on their homicide investigation. Following a fatality, the wreckage often remains in the roadway for long periods of time due to the investigating agency taking pictures and measurements for criminal and civil purposes. My assignment was not a difficult one. From more than a quarter of a mile away, you could see the many emergency lights flashing from the various emergency vehicles working the scene. Drivers knew they were approaching something serious and the natural tendency was to slow down. However, when people start consuming alcoholic beverages and ingesting drugs, they are no longer able to make the rational and safe decision to slow down.

As I stood there directing traffic, cars were traveling between four and five miles per hour. The expressions on the faces of drivers who passed by that death scene were of shock, horror and disbelief. I was distracted for a brief moment when a fellow officer standing a few yards behind me yelled out a question. I took my eyes off the oncoming traffic for just a few seconds. Then I heard another officer yell, "Watch Out!" I quickly turned my head back toward the slow-moving, oncoming traffic in time to see a yellow Honda Civic heading directly at me. The car was traveling at an estimated speed of 45 to 50 miles per hour. This car came upon me so fast that I only had time to *attempt* to dive out of the way. It was too late. The car plowed into me, throwing me more than 80 feet down the highway. I landed at the feet of another officer working the crash scene.

That officer said I landed like a ton of bricks. He thought I was dead since I made no sound or movement. He thought he was looking at a dead police officer. He did not recognize me at first, due to the swelling of my face caused by the injuries. He soon realized, though, that several years earlier he had been my field training officer when I was a rookie cop.

FIVE

My Injuries

I suffered double compound fractures to both legs, a broken right forearm, broken collarbones, a broken left foot, which was literally snapped in half, and several broken toes on both feet. The drunk driver who hit me continued northbound down the highway for several hundred yards, crisscrossing lanes of traffic and eventually pulling behind a closed business in an attempt to hide his badly damaged vehicle. To further hide from the police, he turned his lights off and sat low in the vehicle. My former field training officer gave chase in his patrol car, not fooled by the drunk driver's attempt to conceal his location. He pulled him from his car and arrested him. Sitting in the passenger seat of the suspect vehicle was a girlfriend as drunk as her boyfriend.

The drunk driver quickly complained of having glass in his eyes. How could this happen? When I was struck, I was propelled into the windshield, thrown up onto the roof, and then back off his car. The windshield was shattered, injuring his eyes. Or so he thought.

He was transported to the emergency room where it was quickly determined that there was no glass in his eyes. The only thing wrong with him was a high level of alcohol in his system, more that twice the legal limit. As the officers transported the drunk driver to jail, he said the most shocking thing: "What's the big deal? Cops know they are at risk when they pin their badges on."

As the officers were escorting the drunk driver from the emergency room, his girlfriend was equally unrepentant and was heard saying, "Why are the police officers treating my boyfriend like some common criminal?" I did not know that I would again hear venomous words from the drunk driver. He returned in a few weeks to torment me in the hospital.

SIX

My Angel

While the drunk driver represented the forces of evil, my story includes an angel. When the officers rushed to my aid that night, a female nurse dressed in full operating room attire appeared at the scene. She told the officers at the crash site she was a surgical nurse and her shift at the hospital had ended. She was on her way home and wanted to help in any way she could. She told them where to apply pressure to slow the bleeding from my wounds and distributed an endless supply of medical gauze from her scrub pockets.

After the paramedics arrived to work on me, the police officers stepped back. When they turned to retrieve the nurse's personal information, she had disappeared.

The officers did not see how the nurse arrived at the crash scene. Did she drive up in a vehicle? She just seemed to appear and start instructing the officers as to first-aid procedures. The officers later stated that the nurse departed just as mysteriously. They never noticed her leaving the crash scene. She simply vanished after the paramedics arrived. But at least officers reported that they saw her. They only described her as wearing green surgical hospital scrubs.

Across U.S. Highway 19, there were approximately 150 patrons from a restaurant standing along the highway's edge observing all that was happening. Most of these patrons had been observing the actions of the emergency and police personnel from the original crash. A couple of the police officers made their way across the highway and started interviewing several of the witnesses. The officers asked these people if they had observed the surgical nurse that was working on me. What type of vehicle did she arrive and depart in, they asked. Not one of them observed a nurse at the scene. They only witnessed police officers working on me until the paramedics returned to help. Who could this mysterious nurse have been?

The police officers later spoke to the paramedics who had arrived back at the scene. Had *they* seen the nurse who was instructing the officers how and where to apply pressure on my body, as well as distributing much-needed medical bandages and sterile gauze? The paramedics all stated that they did not observe a nurse at the scene. Why didn't the paramedics see this nurse? Who could she have been? What was her purpose for being there?

The police department's communications division called area hospitals in an attempt to learn her identity. The hospitals said they didn't know who the surgical nurse could have been. Hospital officials said nurses who work in surgery do not go home in their operating scrubs. The scrubs are left behind so they can be cleaned and sterilized. Nor do nurses leave the hospital with bandages and sterile gauze in their pockets. That would violate hospital policy. The shifts at hospitals end at 11:00 P.M. and midnight, not 2:00 A.M. as this mysterious nurse had indicated to the officers. It was later documented by the police officers in their report, "Due to the disappearance of the nurse, we were unable to ascertain her identity." But I came across a passage in the Bible in Psalms 91:11 (NIV) revealing to me who this mysterious nurse was.

For He will command His Angels concerning you to guard you in all your ways.

SEVEN

Bleeding to Death Before Their Eyes

The paramedics could not locate my pulse, nor could they register my blood pressure. When a paramedic inserted a needle into my arm, the vein collapsed around the needle. I was bleeding to death before their eyes. A paramedic then leaned back on his heels from my lifeless body and told an officer standing over me, "I'm sorry. The officer is dead!"

That officer later told me he started to cry and began pleading with the paramedics, "Do something! Please do something!" In an attempt to restart my heart, the paramedics cut through my uniform shirt and then my bulletproof vest. They prepared to insert a long needle under my chest plate and into my heart to pump in adrenaline. Then the paramedics were going to place electric paddles on my chest to shock me back to life.

Having had many years to think about this, I have come to the conclusion that I have either a fear of large needles or electricity. Before the paramedics inserted that needle, I sat up. I calmly told them I thought my legs were broken and my right arm was broken. If they would be so kind as to help me get over to my patrol car, I would gladly drive myself to the emergency room and get checked out. Obviously, I was in shock.

EIGHT

Emergency Room

The paramedics rushed me to the emergency room, where a doctor frantically worked on me, trying to control the bleeding. At one point five bags of blood were administered into my body simultaneously, but my body was spitting it out quicker than they could pump it in. Doctors told me they ordered towels from the laundry room to be placed on the floor around my bed because they kept slipping and falling in my blood. Standing on these towels helped them maintain their balance while they worked on me.

The medical term "compound fracture" means a bone is broken completely in half, and the broken halves of the bone are pushed through the skin and exposed. The double compound fracture that I had in each leg was in the shin bone area. If you have ever bumped or been kicked in the shin bone you probably remember how painful that can be. Imagine looking down at your legs and seeing the four broken ends of each of your shin bones coming through the skin. There are no words that I can share to describe what I was experiencing at that moment. At some point, I became coherent enough to realize what had happened to my legs. And what I saw terrified me.

NINE

Begging to Die

As soon as the doctors controlled my bleeding, they concentrated on my internal injuries. They ordered a series of Xrays. As the emergency room staff began to wheel me down the hall, I reached out to a fellow officer standing next to my bed and said, "*If you love me as a fellow police officer, please kill me! I can't make it. The pain is too intense. Please kill me. Please just let me die!*" I honestly wanted to die. I couldn't imagine drawing another breath in that amount of pain and I wanted to be put out of my misery.

The Xray technicians did not help. They bent me like a pretzel as they took every imaginable Xray of my body. The entire time I pleaded with them, "Please someone, anyone, please just kill me."

From there I was moved to surgery. I spent the next sixteen hours in surgery. The only thing holding my legs on below the knees was a small bit of skin and muscle. During surgery, the doctors did their best to realign my bones and to remove road debris and fragments of damaged bone. At the end of the sixteenth hour, the doctors met with my parents in the surgical waiting room. My parents quickly thanked the doctors for saving my life.

The doctors told my parents they did the best they could but I had lost a great deal of blood and my body had been through too much trauma. They didn't think I would live more than a few days. They said that, if by some miracle I were able to survive this horrible crash, when I gained enough strength, they would probably have to amputate both of my legs below the knees. The doctors said they had pieced my legs back together the best that they could, using four stainless steel rods. They were concerned about infection setting in, due to the large amount of road debris and the gaping wounds to each of my shins. The doctors warned my parents that in all probability I would not leave a wheelchair, nor walk on my own again.

TEN

God's Personal Message

Normally the news that their twenty-two-year-old son may not live more than a few more days would be more than parents could bear. This wasn't the case with my mother. She had already been told by God that I would be okay. Draw your own conclusions after you hear what happened to her five years before my crash.

I was a junior in high school and my mother was at home cleaning. This particular day my mother told me she did something she had not done before while she worked around the house. She turned on the television! On that particular day she turned on a program called *The 700 Club* hosted by Pat Robertson. During this particular segment of his show, Mr. Robertson was "having a word of knowledge."

Mr. Robertson asked the viewing audience to stop and pray with him from their homes if they had children struggling with school, health, or difficulties in general. My mother was concerned for me because I was having a difficult time with Spanish. I couldn't get it, and my grades were reflecting just how far away I was from getting it. My mother stopped her cleaning, sat on the edge of the bed, and bowed her head in prayer, asking God to help me with my studies. What Mr. Robertson said next caused my mother's heart to skip a beat. Mr. Robertson stated, "There is a mother out there who is praying for her son, Mark. God has told me to tell you that He will take care of him. Mark will be okay." My mother thought about what Mr. Robertson had said and thought that it *couldn't* have been directed to her. She was praying for my studies in Spanish to improve and Mr. Robertson was saying, "God will take care of Mark." Certainly that had to be directed to a mother with a son named Mark in serious trouble, not one struggling in Spanish class. My mother dared not share what happened that morning for fear of being thought crazy. She put it out of her mind and soon forgot about it.

Five years later my parents owned a motel on Clearwater Beach in sunny Florida. There came a knock at the office door at about 3:00 A.M. My mother sat up in bed, awoke my dad and told him, "Get dressed quick. Mark has been hurt." My dad tried to calm her fears by reminding her this was the third time someone had come to the motel office in the past hour wanting extra towels or toilet paper. This latest interruption of their sleep was going to be no different than the last three. Dad told my mother to go back to sleep and he would provide what the guest needed and be back shortly. But Mother was already getting dressed. As my dad answered the door, he was greeted by a Clearwater police officer advising him I had been hurt at work.

As my parents made their way to the hospital, my mother feared the worst. Her mind was racing a thousand miles an hour. She felt their car was going barely faster than a crawl. She heard a voice as loud and clear as if someone were sitting in the back seat of the car. She knew it was God's voice, telling her, "I will take care of him." The prayer that Mr. Robertson prayed five years earlier as she sat on the edge of the bed came back to her memory. My mother knew the meaning of that prayer now. It had nothing to do with my having problems in a Spanish class. God was telling my mother five years early that He was going to take care of me now. My mother said she had a peace come over her. And yet, unto this day, I still can't speak a word of Spanish.

ELEVEN

Intensive Care

If you have been blessed with physical health and not had to experience the inner workings of a hospital, you may not be familiar with the unit where some of the most critical of patients are sent. Many of these patients will never regain their strength and many die in intensive care.

I was sent to the intensive care unit after surgery because I wasn't expected to survive, but I feel God had other plans for me. I awoke from my comatose state two days after the horrific crash. As I gained consciousness, the light in the room seemed bright to me. I couldn't make out who was in my room, but I recognized the voices of my parents. I wasn't sure where I was until I heard the distinct sounds: the beeping of intravenous machines pumping fluids in my body, the whisper of oxygen being pumped up my nose through two tubes, and heart-rate monitors. I had heard these sounds in the past when I conducted criminal investigations for victims of serious crimes. Never did I believe that someday I, too, would be hooked to these machines, clinging to life.

After hearing those machines I knew I was in the hospital, but I still didn't know why. As a police officer, the thought of being shot while on duty crossed my mind on occasion. Could this be what happened? I gathered my strength and asked my parents, who I still couldn't see, "What happened to me?" My mother's voice responded, "Honey, you have been in an accident." *An accident*, I thought, *I don't remember an accident*. I then asked, " Was anybody else hurt?" My mothers voice replied, "No, you were the only one hurt." I believe I fell back into unconsciousness for awhile because I remember awakening to the sounds of the critical-care machines again and wondering if I had been shot while on patrol. I didn't remember what my mother explained to me. I awoke again later and I spoke out, hoping that somebody would hear me, "Was I shot?" "No dear, you were hit by a car," my mother replied. I thought perhaps I had caused an accident. I responded back to the direction of my mother's voice, "Was it my fault?" My mother told me, "No, a drunk driver hit you. You are going to be okay!" I again fell back into unconsciousness.

When I awoke once again in intensive care, my vision was clear. I looked around my room. I was able to see the critical-care machines that made beeping and hissing noises throughout the night. I saw that my right arm was in a large plaster cast. My left hand was bandaged with lots of gauze and Ace bandages. Both my legs had plaster casts on them running from my toes to my hips. I saw what appeared to be large blood stains on the front of the casts where the wounds underneath were still bleeding. For the first time it hit me. I was in serious trouble. I was scared. *What happened to me? I don't have time to lie around in the hospital! In just a few weeks I am scheduled to play in the annual high school alumni football game being held at my high school,* I thought to myself.

The alumni football game was a full-contact football game held every year between Clearwater High School and our big rival, Largo High School. If you were a graduate from either school who had played on the football team, you could play in the alumni game. There were some guys who hadn't played since high school and there were those who went on to play college and professional ball who returned for the alumni game. If you were willing to put on pads and play full-contact football, you were welcome. I had played every game since graduating.

As I lay in bed, I thought over and over, *How am I going to be ready to play with all these injuries?* I also wondered when I would be healthy enough to return to work. I never doubted that I would return and do what I loved.

As I continued to scan the hospital room to familiarize myself with my surroundings, I saw something bizarre to my right. There on a little table next to my bed was a book. The book had been placed in an upright position so I would see it. This book was about angels and the author was Dr. Billy Graham. I wasn't sure why this book was in my room. Maybe one of the intensive-care nurses left it in my room by mistake. Why was it sitting on the table in an upright position? I couldn't pick it up since both my arms were immobilized in casts and bandages. Maybe my parents left it in the room?

A short time later a male nurse from the intensive care unit came into the room to check on me. He was glad to see that I was awake and able to talk. I asked him what happened. He said I had been hit by a drunk driver while directing traffic. He told me I had serious injuries to both of my legs and right arm. Doctors would be in soon to explain more about my injuries.

I was overcome with intense pain throughout my body and noticed my scalp was itching badly. The nurse told me that I had dried blood on my scalp and that caused itching. He prepared a pan of warm water and gave me my first of many bed baths. "We're going to make you squeaky clean and powdery crisp," he said. After the bath, he rubbed baby powder on my back. The cool sensation of powder on my skin was refreshing and the itching subsided. The nurse asked if I wanted a shot of pain medicine. I told him I didn't like taking medicine, not even as much as aspirin, and that I would pass on the shot. He told me that I would probably change my mind.

Then I asked him about the book in my room. He assured me that it wasn't his, but he would check to see if one of the other nurses left it in my room. He doubted it because the nurses were so busy. They didn't have time to sit and read! I soon dozed off into a restless sleep.

When I awoke from my sleep I noticed my parents standing at the foot of my bed. Pain was intense, close to unbearable. It was hard for me to concentrate on conversing with my mom and dad. They must have noticed how much pain I was in because they tried to persuade me to take the pain medicine. It was getting more difficult to refuse as the day progressed.

I thanked my parents for the book on angels in my room. To my surprise, they said they did not leave any book. My mother picked it up to see if anyone had written a note inside. There was a note, handwritten, inside the cover of the book. There wasn't a name, though, just a scripture verse from the Bible, the book of John.

> *When he heard this, Jesus said, "This sickness*
> *will not end in death. No, it is for God's glory so*
> *that God's Son may be glorified through it."*
> John 11:4 (NIV)

At the time, I didn't realize how important and personal that scripture would become to me.

Later that afternoon my doctor visited and told me he was going to order morphine so I could rest more comfortably. I objected and told him I didn't want the medicine in my body. The doctor told me that I was doing myself more harm than good by rolling around in bed, trying to cope with the pain. By doing this, I could bend the pins in my legs and complicate things. He ordered the nurses to administer the morphine shots every four hours whether I liked it or not. Shortly after the doctor left, one of the nurses came into my room with an injection in her hand. I could hear another patient screaming and moaning from pain, so I asked the nurse to give him my morphine. He sounded as if he needed it more than I. My plea fell on deaf ears; before I knew it, the morphine was flowing through my veins.

I'll never forget the sensation I felt after that shot. It was as if someone pulled a warm blanket over my body, from the top of my head to the bottom of my feet. I sensed that everywhere this make-believe blanket passed over my body, pain disappeared. For the first time after regaining consciousness, I was without pain. How could I have been so stubborn? Why was I refusing those wonderful shots? I vowed to never, ever, act like Superman and refuse a pain shot again. Bring on the needles!

The next day the doctors met with my parents. It was now three days after the crash. The doctors informed them that my legs were very badly damaged and I was facing a critical time in the recovery process. The doctors told them the chance of infection setting into both of my legs was a real threat. The possibility of losing my legs or even my life was real. The next few days would prove critical in how my body fought off any infection and reacted to the trauma. The doctors removed a lot of road debris and fragments of bone from the shin area of both of my legs. There would be several more surgeries to remove frag-mented bone still floating around in my legs. The doctors were concerned that a piece of fragmented bone could cut an artery or vein, causing serious complications. I spent several weeks in the intensive care unit. I endured another operation to remove bone fragments from my legs. This was the start of a long and trying stay in the hospital. My life would never be the same.

TWELVE

Orthopedic Floor

After three weeks in intensive care, the doctors felt I was stable enough to be moved to the orthopedic unit. This was a boost to my morale. The medical staff must have seen some signs of improvement for me to be moved! I had limited visitors in the intensive care unit but now anyone who wanted could come and say hello.

My healing was slow. I wore two heavy plaster casts up to my hips on both legs. I was also still wearing a plaster cast on my right arm from my hand to my shoulder. I could do very little for myself. The days were long and monotonous. I did, however, have a lot of friends stop by over the next few weeks. My room became the most popular room in the hospital because I received many fruit baskets, homemade cookies, snacks, and games from friends and family. The nurses and their assistants could always find something good to eat, or at night when it was slow, an interesting board game to play.

There were many things to adjust to during my hospital stay. One of the most difficult adjustments was hospital food. To help me return to a normal routine, my parents would often bring lunch or dinner from a favorite restaurant.

I also had to adjust to a lack of activity throughout the day. Days and nights ran together. I had a lot of time to think about my future and my struggle. There were times I was scared so I found myself praying a lot. I knew in my heart God could heal me. He created me, so certainly He could heal me. I just couldn't understand at the time why God would allow this to happen to me. I was one of the good guys; I wore the "white hat." I asked God on more than one occasion, "Why me, Lord, and why both legs?" It would be quite some time before He revealed those answers to me.

Two things, however, that I never adjusted to were using the bedpan and being bathed by nurses, some as young as I was. One of the most humiliating experiences I endured happened one morning as I was being rolled off the bedpan and propped up on my side. I heard the sound of my privacy curtain being pulled back and the sound of giggling coming from behind me as the nurse's assistants were cleaning me. As I was rolled over onto my back, there were a half dozen candy stripers watching me. They were being taught how to clean and take a patient with long leg casts off a bed pan.

Candy stripers are young girls volunteering at hospitals who wish some day to become nurses. I was humiliated. I felt so bad that I soon found myself not wanting to go to the bathroom because I knew it meant I might be used as some sort of teaching aid. I did not want to bare my broken and mangled body to the world. I decided I would hold my urges until the midnight shift arrived. I figured that during the graveyard shift, there wouldn't be any young women to giggle behind my back. I don't think the midnight shift personnel appreciated my decision in giving them the unpleasant job of removing me from the bedpan each night, but I was trying to hold onto the little bit of dignity I had left.

Another difficult ritual was my morning bed bath. The first month in the hospital I was without the use of any of my limbs. I was dependent upon everyone else for everything. I couldn't bathe myself, brush my teeth, nor feed myself. That daily morning ritual never got easier. I was usually awake by the time the day shift arrived at 7:00 A.M. The nurse would bring me a warm washcloth and wipe my face. She would check the bag hanging from the side of my bed to measure the fluids that had drained during the night. She would ask how I was feeling and then administer pain medicine. The first month it seemed I needed pain medicine each time the nurse asked. I was in constant pain from some area of my body. I received so many shots of morphine and other drugs that both sides of my buttocks were black and blue. Eventually, the nurses had to start administering shots to the tops of my thighs, just above my casts.

Once my medicine was administered, a nurse's assistant would bring in breakfast. The hospital food was the most bland and unattractive food that had ever crossed my lips. I would often try to guess what the meal was before the nurse's aides had a chance to tell me what it was. I started losing weight, weight that I didn't have to lose. The doctors became concerned enough that they put me on a high fat and protein diet. The only saving grace was that my parents brought me milk shakes at night.

Once breakfast was hand fed to me and the breakfast tray taken away, a nurse would come in to bathe me. There was one particular nurse the age of my mother who volunteered to bathe me in the morning, which made it a lot easier. On her days off, it was a roll of the dice as to who would be assigned that duty. Male nurses were not as common as they are today. Most of the time it was a young nurse that was as embarrassed giving the bath as I was in receiving it.

The time spent between breakfast and lunch was probably the most boring. Visitors would come in during the evening hours after their work day was through. I would often spend that morning time thinking, praying, and watching television. I couldn't read books or magazines because I had no way of turning the pages since both my hands were immobilized. The nurses were busiest during the day shift so I only spoke to them if they came into my room to administer drugs, check my vital signs, or to roll me onto my side to protect me from bed sores.

At times I was scared about my future. At times I became angry at the drunk driver who ran me over. And at times I directed my anger at God for allowing this to happen to me. On occasion I would ask God the difficult questions that were swimming around in my head. "What did I ever do to deserve this?" "Why both legs?" I was frustrated and confused about a lot of things. I found myself on occasion throwing "self-pity parties." It seemed, however, each time I was enjoying the "pity party", God would reveal to me someone in the hospital that was dealing with a tougher battle than I. God would keep me in line with an occasional reality check. I must say that although I didn't throw a lot of "pity parties," when I did, I was a great host.

The evening hours were easier to handle because I would see family and friends. Talking to my friends was bittersweet. I loved the company, but it was difficult to hear about exciting things like vacation plans, promotions, or intriguing cases. When the visitors were gone, I was alone with my thoughts and fears and the frustration of being confined to bed. The time of year only compounded my frustrations: Thanksgiving and Christmas were just around the corner. I knew in my heart that I was going to be spending the holidays in my hospital room.

THIRTEEN

Holidays in the Hospital

I was excited for my visitors, hearing how they were preparing for the holidays and get-togethers with their families. But when the visitors were gone and I was alone again, my heart ached as much as my mangled legs. The hospital staff told me how the city was stringing up Christmas lights and how much it was starting to feel like Christmas. When I heard the staff talk about Christmas parties, I would sink a little deeper emotionally. I couldn't even look out the window in my room since I was confined to bed. All I could see from my bed when I looked toward the window was a brick wall with a small ledge on it. It was a gathering place for the local pigeons. I eventually was able to recognize them from their different markings. I soon had names for each one of them. What a place to be for the holiday season!

I did win a holiday gift, however. One afternoon, the phone that was connected to my bed rail started to ring. I was startled by the sound. I thought that my family and friends were aware of how difficult it was for me to grasp things. So I couldn't imagine that they would be calling. I was finally able to position the receiver up to my ear and brace it in the crook of my neck with my chin. The voice on the other end was that of a relatively young female. She exclaimed how lucky I was to have just won three free dance lessons from a famous dance studio! She went on to say how my phone number had been randomly selected from the phone book by their computer and I was entitled to the free dance lessons. I was shocked.

I asked the caller who she really was, thinking this had to be a friend of mine playing a joke. The lady caller repeated her claim of free dance lessons and my luck in winning the grand prize in their random drawing. I realized this was no joke. The caller was serious and had absolutely no idea that she was talking to a patient in a hospital.

I explained to her that she had, in fact, contacted the orthopedic floor of a hospital and that I was a patient suffering from serious injuries to both of my legs. I told her that I might very well lose the legs that just won the free dance lessons. I then asked her how she got the number to my room. There was a long silence on the other end of the line. Her voice then started to crack and she cleared her throat. As she fought back tears, she quickly apologized and said she had no idea who she was calling. She had just started working for this solicitation company and was given a list of numbers to call in hopes of attracting potential customers for the dance studio. Then she began crying on the other end of the line. She again apologized for the call and assured me that this was the last call she was going to make because as soon as she hung up the phone she was going to quit. From the tone of her voice, I honestly believe she did.

After that call, I sank into a state of depression. I felt as if I had just been slapped in the face. It was just another reminder as to how physically messed up I was. I remember uttering to myself, "What next?"

My spirits were temporarily lifted a day before Thanksgiving when several officers from the police department walked into my room, carrying a large basket full of food. There was a ham, cheese, crackers, fruit, a sausage roll, and a bottle of non-alcoholic champagne. This basket was so large that it took two men, one on each end of the basket, to carry it. The staff on my floor appreciated the gift as much as I did. There always seemed to be something good to eat in my room.

As Christmas approached, you could see the personality changes in the staff and visitors. Their moods were becoming festive. Even the grinches were in a good mood. Church youth groups would visit. They walked up and down the hallways singing Christmas carols. I remember a visit from the youth pastor and seven youth from the local

Baptist church a month before Christmas. They had brought in an artificial four-foot Christmas tree and decorated it with a paper ornament for each day of the month leading up to Christmas. What made it even more special was the fact that the youth from the church had made the ornaments. Written on each was a different Bible verse of encouragement. They had also decorated the tree with Christmas lights and a star. They placed the tree in the corner of my room, toward the foot of my bed so I could see the tree without having to move or strain my body. The youth and that pastor will never know how much that tree and those Bible verses meant to me. That little tree was my Christmas that year.

The next day, eight officers from my police department completed the midnight shift and decided to pay me a visit before going home. Most hospitals have a rule about how many visitors a patient may have at one time in their room. I can assure you the number is not eight. But my eight visitors wore uniforms and carried guns. Not too many hospital employees question police officers walking through the hallways. Since I was the only patient in the double room, it did not appear cramped. What a wonderful surprise to see the men and women from the squad. Those officers were special to me. We had formed a strong bond by working together for many months on the night shift. Here they were, all together, stopping in to say hello. It really started my day off right.

The last officer who entered the room closed the door behind him so as not to disturb other patients. We were swapping war stories, cracking jokes and having a wonderful time when the head nurse for that day paid me an unexpected visit. She was an older women who had a reputation as a no-nonsense, by-the-book type. She ran the nurses station with an iron fist. I had met her a year or so ago while I was conducting an interview with a motor vehicle accident victim in the emergency room. I had personally witnessed that day how she came about the nickname "Nurse Ratchet," taken from the character in the movie *One Flew Over The Cuckoos Nest*: She yelled and screamed at another nurse in the emergency room that day, bringing the young nurse to tears. She came in and witnessed my friends gathered around the room. You could actually see blood rise to her face, causing her head to turn orange, then fire-truck red. Her face was more colorful than the multicolored star on the top of my Christmas tree. Nurse Ratchet bellowed out, "What are all these people doing in this room?" The first thing that came to mind and escaped my mouth was, "Visiting!" She wasn't impressed with my answer. She hissed, squeaked, and then rumbled aloud, "You three, get off that bed, and you in the wheelchair, quit spinning around like that and get out of that chair. There are too many people in this room. We have rules in this hospital about visiting, only three visitors at one time."

The officers showed restraint that morning. None of them lost their cool or made a sarcastic response back to Nurse Ratchet, but that was about to change. When she spotted my little Christmas tree sitting in the corner, she pulled the plug from the wall and examined the cord, looking for a sticker from the hospital maintenance department to indicate it had been inspected and deemed safe! When no such sticker was visible, she yelled, "This is an unsafe tree and I will have it removed until it is inspected and certified by the hospital. Do you understand me?" I wondered how anyone could be in such a bad mood so early in the morning. One of the officers quietly shut the door to my room and guarded the entry so no uninvited visitors could join us. The officers were okay with her attitude up to a point. But when Nurse Ratchet threatened to remove my Christmas tree, they decided it was time to make a small adjustment in her attitude. This is where I have "selective memory" as to what was said. The officers made it clear that they were not intimidated by her, nor were they going to allow *anyone* to remove my Christmas tree. They suggested she call someone in the maintenance department to immediately inspect the plug on the lights. They were not leaving the room until after this inspection. I had never seen Nurse Ratchet speechless before. She was silenced. She quickly left the room. I thought to myself, *Oh great! You guys get to leave, I'm stuck in this bed, flat on my back, and unable to run away.* I could just see her putting my bedpan in the freezer. About fifteen minutes later, a gentleman from the maintenance department arrived to look at the end of the plug to my Christmas lights. He declared the tree safe, and with that, my electric cord received the famous "Sticker of Approval" notifying all the "Nurse Ratchets" of the world that all was well. The officers had saved my tree. I don't remember Nurse Ratchet ever coming to visit again.

FOURTEEN

Surgeries

During my hospital stay, I had several operations. Surgeons removed road debris and bone fragments from my legs. Bone grafts were completed on both legs, including surgery on my right hip to remove bone for the grafts. I had painful skin graft surgery performed on both legs to close holes in my shins where the bones exploded through my skin upon impact. I had two operations on my right arm to insert metal plates. Little did I know this was only the beginning of the surgeries.

Since the beginning of December, I had been experiencing a lot of pain in the palm of my left hand. There was a cut caused by impact with the windshield. The doctors had cleaned and sutured the deep, jagged cut in the emergency room but pain remained. My fingers were now starting to pull in toward my left palm and I couldn't straighten them without experiencing shooting pain from the incision. I told my doctors something was wrong with my left hand. Maybe they missed some road debris or glass before suturing the wound. The doctors examined the hand and decided scar tissue was forming. As the days passed, the fingers on my left hand were being drawn even tighter into a fist until I could not straighten them at all. So the surgeons worked on my left palm. They found a large piece of glass from the windshield of the vehicle that hit me. The surgery was a success, I regained the use of my hand and my fingers eventually returned to their normal position. However, as I recovered, I was without use of either hand again. My right arm and hand were still in a large cast and now my left hand was completely bandaged. I was dependent upon everyone else for everything again!

FIFTEEN

A Visit from the Drunk Driver

A couple days after the surgery on my hand, a nurse came into my room and told me the driver of the vehicle that ran over me was in the hospital lobby wanting to talk with me. The nurse asked, "Do you want to talk to him or should security escort him off hospital property?" Without thinking, I said it was okay to talk with him. Then I thought, *What have I done?* I couldn't believe I said it was okay for this man to come to my room.

I was so full of anger and hatred! How could I have given permission for him to see me? I had homicidal thoughts. Maybe I could lure him close enough to my bed so I could choke him with the phone cord. Then I remembered I had no use of my hands. A great plan foiled!

I could feel anger boiling within my soul! Then the Lord spoke to me as if someone were standing next to me. The Lord said, "Forgive him!" I replied, "Forgive him? I don't know if I'll ever walk again. I want to kill him. How can I forgive him?" Again, as if He were standing next to me, I heard His voice say, "Forgive him!" Now, being the hardheaded person I can be at times, I asked the Lord, "Is it okay to forgive him after I kill him?" Again I heard, "Forgive him!" As tears filled my eyes and ran down my cheeks, I prayed the second most difficult prayer of my life. It went something like this:

"Lord, remove from me the anger I have towards this man. Please give me a forgiving spirit and the right words to say to him."

As soon as the driver stepped into my room, a weight was lifted from my shoulders. Anger and bitterness disappeared. Peace came over me. As that young man entered my room, he never once made eye contact with me. He seemed eaten up with guilt. He pushed a small chair next to my bed. As he sat down, his head was bowed and his eyes were fixed on the floor. He never looked up. He said in a solemn and low tone, "I don't think it was my fault. You had no business standing in the road directing traffic!"

As I look back on that moment, I realize if God had not taken the anger I had toward that young man, his statement could have been his death sentence. I'm sure, somehow, I would have found a way to kill him. But, instead, God spoke through me to the young man. I said, "Kenneth, before you leave this room today I want you to know something. I don't hate you. I hate the decision you made to get behind the wheel of your car and drive in the condition you were in. I want you to remember I love you, and will be praying for you!" Kenneth was stunned at what he heard me say. He quickly left my room.

I have never had the opportunity to speak to Kenneth again. But, when God brings him to my mind, I pray for him. On my own, I was not capable of saying what I said. I'm not really sure why I said the things I said. What I do know is that God spoke to Kenneth and God spoke to me as well. I came across a scripture not long after that meeting that spoke to my heart.

> *Get rid of all bitterness, rage and anger,*
> *brawling and slander, along with every form of*
> *malice. Being kind and compassionate to one*
> *another, forgiving each other, just as in Christ*
> *God forgave you.*
>
> Ephesians 4: 31-32 (NIV)

I realize that forgiving someone who has wronged you terribly is not easy. To release all anger and bitterness is something to pray about and work toward.

SIXTEEN

Welcome to Medieval Times

Following that memorable visit, I underwent several more operations to remove additional road debris and bone fragments from my legs. I was starting to feel discomfort in the area of the four stainless-steel pins that had been inserted through my legs. The pins were spaced evenly below my knees, with the ends of the pins protruding several inches out both sides of my legs. The purpose of the pins was to keep the shin bones aligned while new growth took place. The pins had been in my legs for two months and my skin was starting to adhere to them, so the doctors decided to remove the pins.

I had endured a half dozen surgeries since my short stay in the hospital so I figured, "What's a few more?" If this surgery would ease the discomfort I was experiencing around the pins, I was eager to have it done.

That evening, the doctor came into my room to check the circulation in my legs. I asked him when I was scheduled to have the pins removed. He said he would do it in the morning. I visualized the type of machinery he would use to remove the pins and assumed it was state-of-the-art equipment.

That night, I prayed as I did before most of my surgeries, asking God to give me the strength to get me through. The next morning I was awakened by the nurse with a warm washcloth and my morning breakfast. I finished my bed bath and was anxious for the surgical personnel to arrive with their stretcher on wheels. I was curious why no one from the surgical department came to visit me as they had always done the night before my other surgeries. They usually checked vital signs and instructed me not to eat or drink anything past midnight. Maybe they didn't feel it was necessary since I was now a professional patient? Maybe they were busy and forgot?

Morning faded into afternoon and still no word from the surgical staff or my doctor. A nurse's assistant brought lunch. I told her I was scheduled for surgery and wasn't allowed to eat or drink anything. She apologized and said no one told her that I was scheduled for surgery. Shortly after that, the nurse assigned to my room came in looking confused. She asked who told me I was scheduled for surgery. I explained that my doctor would be removing the pins in my legs today.

The nurse was unsettled by my news and said that the doctor had not informed her, or nurses on the other shifts, of my surgery. She said she would call him right away. She hurriedly left my room to make her calls and I could almost see steam rising from her head as she departed.

A short time later the doctor paid me a visit and asked me if I was ready to have the pins removed. I asked him how long the procedure would take. He told me he wasn't going to remove the pins in surgery, but in his office on the first floor of the hospital. *Wait a minute*, I said to myself. *How is he going to remove these pins without putting me to sleep?* I asked the doctor how the pins would be removed. He told me he had a special piece of equipment to zip the pins right out. Since I was going to be awake, I asked if it was a painful procedure. The doctor flippantly replied as he left my room, "No. It's never hurt me yet!"

As the hospital orderly began to wheel me to the doctor's office, my mother met me halfway down the hall. I told her I was on my way to my doctor's office to have the pins in my legs removed. A look of confusion came across her face. She asked the orderly if this procedure wasn't usually performed in surgery. The orderly said he wasn't sure, but not to worry: The doctor was going to take *good* care of me! The look of confusion on my mother's face was replaced with a look of terror. When we arrived at my doctor's office, there were many patients waiting. Many had their arms or legs in casts. As I was wheeled into the office, my mother was instructed to wait in the hallway.

The first thing I saw was a large surgical room light mounted on wheels. I then saw my doctor and a nurse in full operating scrubs complete with masks, hats, and gloves. There was a third person in the room, a male orderly standing off in the corner, a different orderly than the one who delivered me to the doctor's office. This orderly looked as if he could have played pro football or been a bouncer at a bar.

For the first time in days, I got a glimpse of my legs, my skin and the pins. I noticed the skin was red around the pins. When the nurse finished removing small sections of the cast, the doctor began to spray a solution over one side of the pins. I asked why he wasn't putting the solution on both ends. He told me he was putting the solution on the ends that would be pulled through the leg, so no infection would be pulled through. At that moment, I knew this was not going to be pretty. But I still had hope that the surgical equipment used to remove the pins would prevent pain.

The doctor then asked the nurse for the drill. She handed him a bundle of sterile towels wrapped around and concealing something bulky. The doctor peeled back several layers of the towels until the drill was exposed. When I saw it, I became sick to my stomach. Could this be some sort of joke? Could I possibly be on the Candid Camera show? I had seen this type of drill when I took wood shop in high school. This state-of-the-art piece of equipment was nothing more than a hand-held, hand-powered drill!

When the doctor clamped the drill onto one end of the first pin, the pain shot through my leg so intense and deep I felt I would loose consciousness. I had never felt such pain. As he pulled the pin out of my leg, all I could do was scream. The nurse had the same look of terror as my mother had a few minutes earlier. As my screams became louder, I tensed up and my body convulsed with the pain. The orderly was instructed to lie across my chest to pin my body to the bed. The louder I screamed, the faster the doctor cranked the drill with his hand. As the first pin was removed, blood streamed out as if it were being pushed by a pump. The nurse applied pressure with sterile bandages on both holes left behind by the now-removed pin. I felt as if I had stepped back into medieval times. Surely, this couldn't be happening in this day and age.

As the second pin was removed, my vision became blurry and I felt dizzy. I thought I was going to die. I pleaded with the doctor to stop. "Let the pins stay in. I don't care. Just stop what you're doing!" Each time another pin was removed, the nurse would move down to a new set of holes and apply pressure to control the blood that was pumping onto the bed and floor. As I continued to scream in pain, the doctor tried to calm me by saying, "Hang in there, only five more pins left. As soon as this is over, I'll buy you a drink."

I wanted to choke him. Didn't he realize it was because of "drinks" that I was in this condition? As the second-to-the-last pin was removed, I slipped into a fog, coming in and out of unconsciousness. When that pin was removed and the doctor saw the state I was in, he said to his nurse, "Maybe we should give him something for the pain!" It seemed to take a lifetime for that medicine to arrive. As soon as the nurse withdrew the needle from my rump, he started to remove the eighth and last pin. He didn't have enough compassion to give the medication time to work before he started his torturous practice again. I passed out before the eighth pin was completely removed. My mother, out in the hallway, was listening to the screams coming from the office and became so upset she ran out of the hospital in tears. She later told me most of the patients who were waiting out in the hallway couldn't handle sitting there, either, listening to me beg the doctor to stop what he was doing. They left as well.

When I awoke, the pain medicine had started to take effect. I wanted to go back to my room and be left alone. No such luck. My next stop was the Xray room. The doctor was now concerned that the bones might not be in the correct alignment after removing the pins. He ordered Xrays to check.

Once I was back in my room, the nurse came in and asked if there was anything I needed. I had her tell the desk in the front lobby that I was not up for visitors for the remainder of the day. I wanted to be alone and sleep. I had the nurse cancel my dinner and close my door. I was done for the day.

The next morning, an orderly arrived with a stretcher and informed me that my doctor wanted to meet me down in the Xray department to take some views. That sounded odd. Why would my doctor be in the Xray department? Doctors don't usually stand with you while Xrays are being taken. When I arrived, my doctor told me it appeared that the alignment of my shin bones was not as good as he would like. He wanted to make a few adjustments. I figured that making a few adjustments would be easy, but then, that's what I had thought about the pins.

He went to work, right there in the Xray area. He cut a pie-shaped wedge out of the side of my cast, and then raised my leg up to his chest, placing the bottom of my foot firmly against his chest. He manually moved the two broken ends of my shin bone into what he thought would be a better alignment. I could hear crunching noises and the pain was horrific. Once he felt he had the proper alignment, his assistant re-plastered the area of cast that had been removed. This procedure was performed on both legs. After both legs were re-aligned, he Xrayed both legs again and I was returned to my room.

I hadn't fully recovered from the events of the previous day and I was being tortured again. My legs were now bleeding through the cast. I started to feel sick to my stomach. Shooting pains ran up my legs and I was sweating as if I had played a game of full-court basketball. I quickly rang for my nurse and asked her for pain medicine. She told me that the doctor did not want me to receive any pain medicine until he reviewed the latest Xrays.

I tried to lie as still as possible and prayed the pain would subside. I hoped the doctor would give the okay for the nurse to administer a pain shot. I knew it would be only then that I would have a chance of becoming comfortable enough to sleep. Outside my room I could hear the distinct sound of a stretcher with what sounded like a loose or wobbly wheel being pushed down the hallway. I felt sorry for the patient who was going to be hoisted onto that stretcher and whisked off to surgery. It could only mean a painful recovery for someone. At least I was through with my torture for the day.

As soon as the nurse administers my pain medicine I can relax, I thought. The sound of the stretcher with the wobbly wheel grew louder as it drew closer. I thought the patient across the hall was being prepped for surgery, the poor guy. I knew the first two days after surgery were the worst. *I'm glad it's not me this time, going down to surgery*, I thought. Just about that time there was a faint knock on my door. I immediately thought, *Oh no. Now I have to entertain a visitor. Maybe if I explain what I went through, they will understand and not be upset with me.* As I rolled over onto my back I was greeted by my doctor's assistant. "What now?" I asked. The doctor still didn't like the alignment of my bones and wanted me brought back down to make another adjustment. *I* was the one placed on the stretcher with the wobbly wheel. Again the doctor cut a pie-shaped wedge out of my casts, and again, he bent my bones into a different alignment on both legs. I was returned to my room with the assurance that he would not put me through any more pain today. The nurse had changed my bed sheets when I was gone and the linen felt so cool and refreshing against my sweaty skin. Finally I could be alone. Finally I could get a shot to help ease the pain that permeated every joint in my body. I felt I had been through enough for one day, maybe even a lifetime. I wanted to be alone! Off in the distance I again heard the faint sound of the stretcher with one wobbly wheel being pushed down the hall. Time for a third alignment! And I survived again. Barely.

SEVENTEEN

The Great Escape

One of the highlights of my early stay at the hospital was when I was moved from my bed into a specially equipped wheelchair for a short period of time. This wheelchair could be converted into a stretcher on wheels quickly. If I were to faint or become ill, I could immediately recline back to a flat position with the help from staff.

They prepared me for this big event, first, by dressing me. They helped me put on a pair of gym shorts my mother had modified to fit over the long casts on both legs. My mother also brought in a loose fitting T-shirt the night before my big outing. This was the first time I had clothes on since the crash. I was so excited to get out of bed and outside my room.

As the staff placed me in a sitting position, I experienced a slight sensation of dizziness. I dared not tell the nurses, so as not to ruin my big day. They wheeled me out of my room and down the hall. There they positioned me and the chair in a remote corner of a pediatric floor. Since this was my first time sitting up since being hurt, I might become dizzy or sick if I were up too long. The nurses reassured me that if I felt lightheaded at all, they would immediately bring me back to my room so I could rest. The goal was to gradually build up my strength in a sitting position.

I felt great. The scenery was a boost to my spirits! Nurses, nurse's aides, and visitors talked with me. I watched the staff and visitors walk up and down the hall and reflected back to time before the crash. Once, I too, could glide around on my legs as they were doing. I was scared that I still might never walk again or even lose my legs completely.

At the end of one hallway was a set of elevators. As I sat there, I noticed a group of four uniformed police officers step off the elevator and walk toward me. Before long I recognized the officers. I had worked with them and when they saw me sitting in a wheelchair, they broke out in big smiles.

They had a lot of questions about my progress. It was noisy in the hall so they asked if they could take me to a quiet spot where we could talk. The nurse hesitated in granting their request since this was my first time being in the new position and they needed to keep a close eye on me. The officers assured her that I would be in excellent hands. If I grew tired, they would personally wheel me back immediately.

Once we arrived at the visiting area, the officers updated me on our police department. I told them how much I missed them and looked forward to visiting the department before long. I told them one day I would arrive unannounced and shock everybody. They looked at each other, then at me. One of the officers said, "Let's go now!" I said, "You guys are crazy. We'll get caught for sure." With that, one officer got the elevator, one kept watch for the nurse, and two others guided me out.

The police department was across the street from the hospital. Soon, I was on my way. I went to the first floor of the hospital with a police escort. We cut through the emergency room to avoid the administrative offices and then outdoors. It was invigorating to smell fresh cool air and feel sunshine on my face. When we arrived at the end of the sidewalk, we had to cross the street. Two of the officers walked into the intersection, blew their whistles loudly, and motioned traffic in all directions to a complete stop. Once all the cars were stopped, they pushed me across the street and through the back door of the police department. This journey took about fifteen minutes.

Once I was safe inside the police department, communications personnel announced over the intercom that I was paying a visit. I was soon surrounded by co-workers and friends. I then realized how much I missed my old life and wanted it back. As I fielded the questions from everyone, two detectives were busy coloring each of my toenails with a red felt-tip marker. When the last toe was painted, Captain Sam Raney walked into the room and asked who had kidnapped me from the hospital. He had received a call from a panicked nurse, wanting her patient back and back now! The doctor was making his rounds and if I wasn't in my room, there would be a lot of explaining to do.

The four officers who brought me to the station returned me. When I saw my nurse again, I told her I had some good news and some bad news. She looked at me and said, "Tell me the bad news, and tell me quick. The doctor is on his way up." I pulled up the sheet that was covering my freshly painted toenails. "You guys are going to get me fired," she shrieked. With that, she ran out of my room. She came back later, purse in hand. Then she poured the contents of her purse onto my bed. She grabbed a bottle of fingernail polish remover and started rubbing my toenails.

The bright red turned a light pink. "What did they put on your toenails:" she asked. I was pretty sure it was a red felt-tip marker. She was really panicked now. The doctor was due in my room at any minute and he would be testing my circulation as part of his visit. If the doctor were to see my toenails painted—and if he found out that I took a trip off of the hospital property—she could be fired.

I told her I would keep the bed sheet over my feet so he couldn't see my toenails. She said he would be squeezing my toes between his fingers to see how quickly the color returned. This is one way to check circulation. With that, the nurse ran out of my room a second time, leaving the contents of her purse all over my bed. In a minute, she returned with a lady from housekeeping, brought in to assist with this unique cleaning project.

While the housekeeping lady scrubbed my toes with an abrasive cleaner, the nurse frantically put the contents back into her purse. The lady from housekeeping used a cleaner that returned my nails to their normal color. Then, the doctor came in. Just as the nurse had explained, the doctor squeezed my big toe between his thumb and fore-finger and watched for the color under my toenail to return. He looked up and said my circulation was still good. He then paused and started sniffing the air around the foot of my bed and asked if my room had just been cleaned. I told him that housekeeping had scrubbed my floors that afternoon. The doctor bought it. When the nurse came back into my room, she was anxious to hear about the doctor's visit. I assured her that her job was safe.

EIGHTEEN

Bad News from the Doctors

After I had been a patient for a little over three months, the doctors contacted my parents to set up a meeting. I assumed they wanted to discuss my future treatment and care. Both of my legs were still in casts and my right arm was in a cast as well.

My parents arrived at the hospital for the scheduled meeting. My room appeared small with two doctors, both my parents, and several administrators all standing around. I knew something was up when one of my doctors shut the door. One doctor whispered instructions to a nurse to keep all visitors and staff out, while the other doctor sat on the edge of my bed. He reviewed the details of my case and said I was missing approximately an inch of bone in each leg. The inch gap that I had in both of my shin bones should have been getting smaller and filling in with new bone. My shin bones were not producing new growth and appeared damaged beyond repair. I was sickened, "What do you mean, damaged beyond repair?" "That can't be. I have to get back to work," I told them. I looked toward my parents. For the first time in my life, I saw an expression of fear and complete helplessness on my father's face. My mother was fighting back tears. The hospital administrators had their heads bowed, staring at the floor.

The doctors went on to say I should start thinking about letting them amputate both my legs. They told me there were many things I could do from a wheelchair. I should accept what happened, turn this page in my life, and start thinking about my future. My mother was now crying uncontrollably. My father had turned white. The doctors continued. They had done all they could for me and it was time to move me to a health center for the remainder of my recovery. I asked why I couldn't stay in the hospital. I had made some wonderful friends on the staff. They had become like a second family. The administrators chimed in and told me the hospital was for acute-care patients, and since I didn't fit that criteria any longer, I was required to move. A flood of emotions surged through my body. I was just told that, in all probability, I was going to lose my legs, which meant losing my career and being crippled for life. Along with that, I was now going to move away from the caregivers I was close to. I was fighting mad! I told the doctors they were never going to amputate my legs! As long as I could move my toes, no matter how slight that movement was, they were never taking my legs from me. My mother ran out of the room and my dad followed behind, hoping to comfort her.

I was told I had to move to a health center. I asked the doctors what a "health center" was. They said it was a place where patients go to recover for short stays of a few months. I couldn't believe they had given up on me. I was twenty-two years old and my whole life was in front of me. I wondered, *Would they be this quick to give up if it were their son or daughter in this hospital bed?* I asked when I was going to be moved out. They told me within a few days. I again reminded them that they would never remove my legs. They did not respond but quietly slipped out of my room.

My mind was racing a thousand miles per hour. I didn't sleep that night. With the change of each shift, nurses, nurse's aides, and orderlies came to wish me luck on my new location. Many had tears in their eyes. I remember praying that night and asking God what was up. Why would He do this to me? I was angry. I reminded God that you can't be a cop without legs. I didn't want to give up my childhood dream. I wanted to return to police work. My anger turned into determination that night. I was determined to prove the doctors wrong. If God didn't want to heal me, I would heal myself.

That next day, I set three goals and wrote them on paper. When my doctors returned, I shared my goals. They

told me I was only setting myself up for more disappointment. I should accept what happened and go on with life.
I was determined to prove them wrong!

The first goal was to walk again on my own two legs.
My second goal was to work as a police officer. No drunk
driver could take that dream away from me. I was determined to get back in uniform patrolling the streets of
Dunedin. The third goal caused the strongest reaction
from my doctors. I felt I was losing control of my future so
I guess a way to strike back at them for giving up on me
was to set a seemingly impossible goal: I vowed someday I
would run in a race.

NINETEEN

Moving to the Health Center

I was set to move to the Belleair East Health Center. I was told it was a new facility where young adults like myself recover from various injuries. I figured I would now have the opportunity to meet other patients my age struggling with recovery. Maybe I could help someone with their struggle or I might be helped. I was determined to be as positive about the move as possible. I didn't want to be the cause of any more pain for anyone who knew me, especially my parents.

On the day of the move, all the nurse's and nurses aides came to my room to wish me well. I felt as if they were my little sisters and I was heading off to college. There wasn't a dry eye in the group, including mine. Those nurses had looked out for me and kept me alive.

I remember some of them stopping by the hospital to see me on their days off. They all went the extra mile, far beyond the call of duty, and became like family. They helped pack my few possessions that moving day. My mother arrived and then a driver from the wheelchair transport company. The gentleman loaded me and my wheelchair into a specially equipped van. My mother followed behind in her car. I asked the driver on our way to the health center what the place was like. He told me it was a new facility and had only been open a few months.

The health center did not appear fancy, a one-story brick building with a small pond and a floating fountain out front. As the driver pulled into the entrance, the sign with the facility's name came into view. I was confused. The sign indicated that we had just arrived at Belleair East Nursing Home. I figured the health center must be around the rear of the complex. When the driver parked the van, I asked where the health center was. I told him I was supposed to go to a health center, where other patients my age were recovering. The driver told me that this was not a health center but a nursing home.

My stomach was in knots. Someone had lied. Why didn't the hospital administrators or my doctors tell me the truth from the beginning? They were shipping me off to a nursing home! Nursing homes had a reputation for being depressing, smelling of urine, places where senior citizens go to die. Why was I here? Was I sent here to grow old and die? I couldn't believe this was happening to me. This was no "health center."

It looked new and clean from the outside, but still, it was nothing more than a nursing home. But I thought maybe there was a health center inside. I could only hope no one had lied. I remembered the promise I made to myself back at the hospital: I wasn't going to get down. I was going to make this move appear positive, if for no other reason than my mother's peace of mind!

As the driver unloaded me from the transport van and pushed me up to the front door, my mother parked her car. She then walked alongside me, holding my hand. As we entered the front lobby, there was no one in sight except for some old people walking aimlessly. We were finally greeted by a lady dressed in what appeared to be a nurse's uniform. She told us the staff was finishing lunch and would be back in a few minutes. The driver had my mom sign some papers and then he left.

I looked around at my surroundings. This was definitely not a health center. There were no other patients my age or even close to it. This was nothing more than a typical nursing home. It was a new and clean nursing home, but nevertheless a nursing home. At least the facility had not taken on the typical musty urine smell. I was trying to keep a positive spirit and attitude. I didn't want my mother to see me down. I knew by the look on her face that this was equally difficult for her.

I still couldn't help thinking, "This is a place where people come to die." I really had to work on maintaining a positive attitude. I was mad at my doctors for sending me off to this place. As my mother pushed me around in my wheelchair, I realized I was probably going to be at least fifty years younger than the other residents. My mother positioned my wheelchair so I could sit and look toward the little pond out front. She pulled up a chair and sat next to me as we waited for the administrator. I looked over and saw tears building in her eyes. I could only imagine what my mother was feeling as we sat there. My heart broke for her.

Instead of voicing my dislike for this facility, I told my mother it wasn't so bad. I tried to point out how clean it was and how nice they kept the grounds. She cried as she told me she had no idea it would be a nursing home. I assured her that everything was going to be okay. I wouldn't be in this place for more than a few months. This helped her a bit, but her tears didn't dry. My mother was heartbroken for me and my situation. That hurt me more than my injuries.

Eventually, we were met by a man who introduced himself as the administrator. He welcomed us and assured us that his staff would make my stay as comfortable as possible. With the paperwork filled out, I was pushed to my new home, a private room I wouldn't have to share with elderly residents. This perk was only obtained after my attorneys battled it out with the insurance company. (I'd had a real education about insurance companies.) Luckily, my union stepped in and retained legal counsel for me. I was grateful for the space and privacy that I would have.

My room had an electric bed so I could raise my head or feet to make myself comfortable. The bed had a triangular handle hanging down above me so I could reach up with my good hand and lift myself when I needed to reposition my body. There was a dresser, a nightstand, and a small television. The room had a small bathroom, similar to what you might find in a hospital room. My mother stayed for a few hours before leaving to return home. I sat in my wheelchair staring out the window for about thirty minutes, deep in thought about my future. I felt *so* alone! I wanted my life back. I wanted to wake up from this nightmare and find myself back in my own home and back to work. Yet I knew that was impossible.

My parents could not provide for my care. It took two and often three people to roll me over to relieve my back from pressure and prevent bed sores. I was still confined to either the wheelchair or the bed, unable to use the bathroom on my own. I couldn't put that burden on my parents. I knew if I had asked them, they would have tried to care for me at home. But as owners of a busy motel, they couldn't take on my care. The motel often ran my parents instead of my parents running the motel. I knew I was in the right place at this time. But I longed for my normal life to return as quickly as possible.

My deep thought was quickly interrupted by a knock at the door. I was greeted by representatives from the nursing, housekeeping, and cafeteria staffs. I was warmly welcomed and given a tour of the facility that I now called home. As we traveled the hallways, I was also greeted by stares from children visiting their parents. I'm sure they had not seen a resident as young, nor as bandaged as I was. I felt as if I were on display. (To this day, it's still hard for me to put on a pair of shorts and go out in public. At times

I'm even a little uncomfortable in shorts around my extended family.)

During the next few weeks I learned to dress myself with one arm and operate the electric bed. I could lower it to be even with my wheelchair, making it easy to slide from the bed to the chair. I was beginning to regain a little more of my independence. I started to feel good about myself since I was finally able to do a few things on my own without waiting for someone to help me.

At breakfast, lunch, and dinner, a staff member would come to my room or locate me in the hallway and wheel me to the cafeteria for my meals. Since both of my legs were still in casts and I couldn't bend my knees, I was unable to sit at the table like everyone else. The staff would wheel me to the table and I would sit with my side facing the food and then reach across my body with one hand to feed myself. It was almost as if I were eating over my shoulder. But that was not the hard part.

What was difficult was sitting in that large cafeteria with all the elderly residents, many of whom were suffering from one form of dementia or another. Many were deteriorating from Alzheimer's disease. It was depressing to sit with a room full of people yet be unable to carry on a conversation. I petitioned to eat in a separate room with the staff. I eventually was allowed to do so, but only after I complained. The administrator was uncomfortable allowing me this extra privilege for fear he would have to allow others to do the same. I convinced him I wasn't like the others. I don't think he ever truly approved of this accommodation for me. But it was great to be able to carry on a conversation with people closer to my age. The fact that I was able to eat with healthy people my own age may not seem like a big deal to most. But it made a big difference to me because I could feel normal for part of the day.

TWENTY

Public Interest

Occasionally, I would get calls from local news-papers interested in doing feature articles about my progress. My story was followed closely by the community and the newspapers would periodically write about how I was doing.

The first article written while I was a patient in the nursing home was published soon after my arrival. A reporter wrote about how my days were spent recovering and how I was able to cope physically and mentally in my new surroundings. I shared with the reporter that my faith in Christ had grown stronger and I found myself reading the Bible more. I tried to think of positive things throughout the day, as well as think about the day I would walk out of the nursing home on my own two legs. I'm not sure the reporter believed what I was saying, but I was glad to read that he wrote accurately what I shared with them that day. This article was placed in the Sunday edition in the religious news section. I assume this was because of the references I made to Christ and the Bible and how I was learning to lean on God through my most difficult time. I would rather have had the article printed in another section of the paper because I think more people would have read it. I've always shared with readers or viewers encouraging words they could hold onto in dealing with their own personal struggles. So I'd hoped to reach as many people as possible.

One of the good things about the article being in the religion section was that it covered the entire front page. The photograph they took of me in my wheelchair as I sat by the pond reading my Bible was in full color. I was hoping this would attract some readers who normally might not read that particular section of the newspaper.

When that paper came out, I received a lot of calls from wonderful people in the community wishing me well. Whenever a newspaper article about my story was published, I would always get calls and visitors. This particular Sunday was no exception. I received get-well cards, cookies, and even pictures drawn by children. A few folks stopped by the nursing home to pay me a visit and bring extra copies of the article for family and friends. On those days, I could see how the community was pulling for me.

However, not everyone is so decent. There are always one or two percent of the population that march to a different drummer. Because of these individuals, law enforcement officers will always have job security.

That Sunday night, I was awakened from a sound sleep by a uniformed police officer from a department near the nursing home. I was startled to see a police officer leaning over me as I awoke. He was shaking me and as I gathered my thoughts, I could also see the nursing home administrator and a few of his staff in the hall outside my room. They whispered quietly among themselves.

The first thing I thought was that there was something wrong with my mother or father. The officer assured me they were fine. My eyes were now focusing more clearly and I was fully awake. I could hear the sounds of police radios squawking outside my room and people walking around on the roof. The officer standing next to my bed informed me that someone had called the nursing home and said, "There is a bomb above the cop's room and it will be going off soon." The officer advised me that they were going to check the entire roof of the nursing home. They also had an explosive-detection dog checking the exterior of the nursing home for anything suspicious.

I never felt threatened that night. I had been to many bomb-threat calls over the years. I knew it was some nut who read the article about me in the newspaper. For whatever reason, maybe just a dislike for police in general, he decided to call in a bomb threat.

The police were at the nursing home for an hour. The officer who awakened me stayed by my side the entire time to keep me calm and to assure my safety. This is typical of police officers all over this country. They will stay by a fellow officer's side through thick and thin. Nothing was found that night and, despite the attempt to frighten me, life went on.

Approximately two weeks later, another area newspaper came to the nursing home and interviewed me. When that article appeared, another bomb threat was called in to the nursing home.

TWENTY-ONE

Life at the Nursing Home

My days at the nursing home ran together. I soon fell into a routine. I knew what each hour of the day would bring, and which families visited their parents, and when. I was a captive audience to the grind and monotony of the day. All the activities and entertainment were geared to elderly residents. Often, I found myself sitting in a corner listening to a small portable radio I kept on my lap.

My favorite pastime back then, as it is today, was fishing. Oh, how I love to fish! Fresh water or salt water, I'll wet a line and bend a pole. So my parents brought me one of my fishing poles. There was a little pond with a fountain in front of the nursing home. I knew there weren't any fish in the pond, but nevertheless, I had to try. Almost every afternoon I would grab my fishing pole in my good hand and balance my little plastic tackle box on my lap. I would have someone push me outside to the spot where the ground started to slope down toward the water. Once I was positioned just right, they would lock the brakes on the wheelchair. I would spend the next few hours casting my rubber worm into that little pond. In all the hours I spent fishing, I never once got a bite, let alone a fish.

That wasn't what was important to me. Fishing was something none of the other residents could do. That made me different and I had to be different! I *had* to be different. They came to this facility to finish their last days on earth. I wanted to walk out of that place and live as many days on earth as I could. I think I feared ending up like them. That's why I had to be different. Besides, maybe there was one big fish in that little pond waiting for me to drop my worm into the right spot.

One of the few things I looked forward to was having Xrays taken of my legs. Each visit, I would pray for signs of new bone growth in my shins. I knew I couldn't stand up until that inch gap was filled with new bone. Sometimes I felt like a prisoner going before the parole committee to see if I was going to regain my freedom. For a year, once every month, it was the same diagnosis: No new growth! Each time, the doctors reminded me that I should accept what happened. They told me how advanced prosthetics were. The doctors told me that if my legs were amputated,

I could gain freedom from the nursing home. I was told on more than one occasion that there was a lot I could do from a wheelchair. Each and every time I would tell them a resounding "NO!"

I remember one afternoon when my mother stopped by for a visit. During the course of the visit, a nurse I had never seen before came into my room. She had been sent to discuss double amputation and the world of prosthetics. She went on to describe how lifelike fiberglass legs look. She explained how mobile I would become with a little practice. She talked as if I had already made the decision to have my legs removed.

My mother eventually ran out of my room crying because of this uninvited nurse from a prosthetics company. I worried about my mother trying to drive home in hysterics. I told the nurse to get out of my room and never come back. If she did, I would personally arrest her for trespassing. I then called my doctor and asked why he had given up on me. Why did he send this nurse to talk about the amputation of my legs? He assured me that he had not sent her. Then in the same breath, he reminded me it had been close to a year and my shin bones were showing no signs of healing. I knew in my heart that the doctors had given up on me ever healing. I figured I had to heal myself.

For the next month, I went on a vitamin kick. My parents brought in every vitamin promoted to strengthen and produce new bone. I took vitamins C, E, potassium, bone meal, and numerous others. I had enough vitamin bottles to fill two shoe boxes. I was probably taking fifteen to twenty vitamins twice or three times a day. My vision became blurry and I experienced stomach cramps. I figured it was a small price to pay to get my bones to heal. One morning as I was getting ready to take my small mountain of vitamins, a nurse walked in. She couldn't believe the number of vitamins I was ready to consume. She immediately confiscated all the vitamins on my tray and the two shoe boxes full of vitamin bottles as well. I received a stern dissertation on how dangerous it is to take so many vitamins at once. It took approximately two to three weeks to get my vision and system back to normal.

Shortly after the seizure of my vitamins, my doctor told me he wanted to try something new. He recommended a doctor in the city of Clearwater who had an assistant known as an excellent "cast man." This person was the best in the area to fit patients like myself with walking casts. If I were to stand and walk, maybe my legs would produce electrical currents within the bone, thus stimulating them to grow and heal. I asked how I would be able to stand, since both of my shin bones were missing an inch of bone. How could my shin bones support me if they were not solid? My doctor said the short-leg casts would have a lip protruding from the top so my knees would rest and not bear weight. *Could that really work*, I thought? I couldn't imagine *how* that was going to work, but I put those thoughts away. I wanted to walk and walk now! I figured if I could start walking now, the remainder of my recovery could be done at home. I called my parents to tell them the good news. I would soon be walking again! I told everybody at the nursing home that I would be walking again and on my way home soon.

The following week dragged until the night before my appointment. I couldn't sleep for the excitement. I was finally going to get rid of these plaster casts and be fitted with fresh short-leg walking casts. I was already starting to plan the remainder of the week. Who would I visit, once I was discharged from the nursing home? I anticipated sleeping in my own bed and enjoying my mother's cooking again. I began to wonder what I could do at the police department while walking in the new casts. Maybe I could start back to work the following week!

When the driver from the transport company came, I shared my good news with him all the way to the doctor's office. As I was wheeled into the waiting area, I was met by my parents, who came to be part of the big day. I thought to myself, *I will soon be leaving this office with my parents and returning to my home. One of my parents can stop by the nursing home, fill out discharge papers and collect the few possessions I have there.* I realized I did not say goodbye to any of the staff at the nursing home. I decided I could call from my parent's home to thank them for all their hard work, although I wished I would have said my good-byes in person. My mind was racing so fast I almost didn't hear the receptionist call my name. I quickly yelled out, "Here I am. I'm Mark Franzman!" The receptionist pushed my wheelchair as my parents followed us back to a room that had an inch of dust from plaster casting on every imaginable surface. My parents chose to stand rather than sit on the dust-covered chairs. In one corner was a contraption that was a combination shop vacuum/ circular handheld saw. I realized that I hadn't seen my legs in over a year. I wondered what they looked like after such devastating injuries.

Terry, the doctor's assistant, introduced himself and we shook hands. I introduced my parents and explained how excited I was to be fitted with the walking casts. Terry said he had reviewed the paperwork and would now remove my casts. He cut a seam down both sides of the casts, used a special tool to pry them apart and then gently started to cut and remove the layers of gauze and cotton that had been used to pad my skin. I noticed a horrible stench coming from the casts. The smell of something rotting soon permeated the doctor's office. My mother covered her nose and I had to force back my gag reflex so as not to get sick from the stomach-turning odor.

Terry made his final cut, which allowed me to see my legs for the first time since the crash. My heart fell to my stomach. My father and mother had to step outside to get a breath of air and to gather their composure. I didn't recognize my legs. Those couldn't be the same legs that propelled me around the high school track. Nor could they have been the legs that carried me down the football field for a touchdown during the homecoming game. These were not the same legs that ran an average of fourteen miles a day while training for sports. The legs I saw were thin, mangled, sore-ridden, and green. Terry looked hard and long at those sorry excuses for legs and then looked me in the eye as if to say, "What happened to you?" before continuing his examination. He wanted the doctor to examine my legs before he did anything further. He exited the room as my parents reappeared and tried to reassure me. All I could do was to stare at these disfigured, green-looking sticks that were now my legs. My hopes of going home and back to work were quickly erased by the vision of my legs. I wondered how I would ever be able to walk again.

The doctor came into the room and introduced himself. He said Terry was given orders from my current doctors to fit me with short leg casts. His exam began. The doctor moved one leg from side to side. It was obvious that there was no fusion of the shin bone. He shook his head from side to side as if he had just been told disturbing news. He examined my other leg in the same fashion. Then he examined my skin. "I'm a experienced orthopedic surgeon," he said. "There is no way that I can allow you to be fitted in short-leg casts. Your shin bones are not solid. If you were to stand up in your condition, you would end up back in surgery. Your bones would come pushing through the skin just as they did the night you were run over. Your legs appear to be rotting from being in the casts for such a long time."

He then asked me how old I was and how long I had been in this condition. I told him I was twenty-three years old and it had been nine months. He told me I was too young to be in a nursing home and that I should have been back to work by now. I asked him why my legs refused to mend. He explained that the shin bones needed new, fresh bone to be introduced to the break area in order to heal. He said that if I were his patient, he would first get my skin healthy. Then he would perform a surgical procedure to open up my hip area and remove bone from my pelvis. He would graft bone he took from my pelvis into the breaks in my shin bones. Next he would run electrical current through my legs to stimulate the shin and grafted bone to eventually become fused and solid again. Unless new bone was grafted into the break areas, my legs would never heal, and I would likely end up losing them.

My mind was about to explode! What should I do? I thought I was finished with surgeries. I was counting on going home today. The doctor told me to think it over and talk with my parents. If I decided to have it done, he would take me on as a patient and perform the surgery.

I fought back tears. I couldn't get the image of my legs out of my mind. I thought about what the doctor had said. "You should have been back to work by now." That was the first positive thing I had heard from *any* doctor in almost a year. I didn't utter one word on the ride back to the nursing home and I didn't sleep all night.

The next day my depression turned into anger. I felt an entire year of my life had been wasted. Why didn't the other doctors mention anything a year ago about bone-graft surgery? If they had, I might have been back to work by now. I decided that a change of doctors was needed if I had any hope of getting my life back. However, I didn't want to make a mistake by choosing the wrong doctor. Enough time had been wasted. I needed a doctor who could get the job done. I didn't know anything about this new doctor. I wasn't even scheduled to see him. I was sent there only to see his assistant. I had to make sure he knew what he was doing.

I began a research project. I had a staff member bring me a phone book, pad of paper, and a pencil. I started calling orthopedic surgeons in the Tampa/Clearwater area. The surgeons I was able to speak with all referred me to Doctor Siek. One doctor in particular told me that if it were his son, he would have Doctor Siek perform the surgery. I was convinced my new doctor would be Gerard Siek, MD. He was, coincidentally, the doctor I had visited the day before.

My parents arranged for my medical charts and reports to be sent over to Dr. Siek. A few days later I had my casts removed again. Since the skin on my legs was in such poor condition, Dr. Siek could not operate immediately. He had me admitted to the hospital so a therapist could work on my skin. Twice a day, I was brought to physical therapy and placed in a Hubbard tank. A Hubbard tank is a large metal whirlpool, big enough for a patient and several therapists to enter at the same time.

I was excited but still angry about the fact that an entire year of my life had been wasted in a hospital and nursing home. But I couldn't change that, so I concentrated on the future. I prayed that God would work through Doctor Siek to heal my legs. Every time I met with disappointment, I asked God to give me the strength to continue. God never let me down! I found great comfort through the prayers and conversations I had with Him.

So it was, finally, time for me to move on. I said farewell to the staff at the nursing home. Some of the residents made a point to wish me luck in surgery. This was going to be one of the most important operations I would undergo. It was comforting to know that there were so many people concerned about me. I knew in my heart that God was going to heal me!

TWENTY-TWO

New Hospital and New Doctor

As I arrived at the new hospital, I was admitted into a semiprivate room. I was excited about the prospect of returning to work someday, but anxious about the pending surgery. I was especially dreading the recovery process. By this time, I knew what to expect. The most difficult time would be the first two days. I've always hated the feeling of losing control of my body. The medications used after surgery are strong. They make me groggy and out of control at first, a feeling that I never learned to enjoy.

I was excited about my first treatment in the Hubbard tank, although I was nervous about the pain I might feel in it. Ever since I had the pins removed from my legs, I had become apprehensive about new treatments. But it felt good to be doing something toward healing. I was getting discouraged sitting around and waiting. Now at least *something* was happening. I was working towards recovery.

When I arrived at the physical therapy room, I noticed a large metal whirlpool that could have passed for a small swimming pool because of its size. The therapist wheeled me to the side of the tank so I could become familiar with the equipment I would be using many hours over the next week. There were whirlpool jets positioned all around the sides of the tank. The water appeared to be about three feet deep. Suspended from the ceiling was a large metal beam with a track attached to it. Above the tank, pulleys hung down and held a stretcher which would be used to place me in the tank. One therapist placed me in the water while the other maneuvered the jets. In seconds the clear, calm water in the tank turned into a swirling, violent pool of water. The smell of chlorine was strong, almost choking me with each breath I took. I saw steam rising from the tank toward the ceiling. Although it smelled, the water was warm and soothing to my legs. I noticed dead skin pulling away from my legs immediately. The therapist in the tank with me started to gently massage my legs with a sponge that was soft on one side and slightly coarse on the other. The massage felt wonderful. For so long, my legs had not been touched! By the end of the therapy session, dead skin from my legs completely covered the surface in the tank. I couldn't believe that amount of dead skin came from two skinny legs!

I visited the Hubbard tank twice a day for almost a week. The skin color of my legs changed from unhealthy green to healthy pink. At the beginning of the second week, I was scheduled for major surgery. I was about to undergo a bone-graft procedure that would eventually allow me to walk again.

Surgery was scheduled for October 19, almost one year to the day of my accident. I was on my way to surgery at three o'clock in the afternoon. I had prayed hard the night before, asking God to allow this procedure to work. A year of my life was now gone because of the careless act of a drunk driver. I didn't want to lose any more time.

Since I had undergone so many operations, the pre-op shot that the nurse administered to me had little affect. I guess my body had started to build up a tolerance toward the narcotics. As I waited on the stretcher, I was wide awake and coherent. I saw my high school football team doctor walk by on his way to his surgery. I called out his name. He slowed down and looked around, wondering who called him, never once looking down at the patient on the stretcher. I again called his name. Finally, he looked down at me and asked if I was going to have the bone graft surgery. I told him I was and he assured me that Doctor Siek was one of the best in the business.

He then asked if I had been administered a pre-op shot. He was curious because I was unusually alert. When I told him when the shot had been administered, he had a look of amazement. He said I must have the tolerance of a bear. He read my chart and wished me luck. After he walked away, he talked to one of the nurses. They both then looked toward me. I knew something was up. The nurse had a quick telephone conversation with someone, and before long, she came over with a syringe in her hand. She told me that she was going to increase the dosage of my pre-op shot. Shortly after receiving that injection, I felt like a bowl of pudding.

Soon a nurse dressed in full operating scrubs walked up and asked me how I was feeling. I could hardly manage to get words out of my mouth, but I told her I was feeling fine. She then asked what procedure I was having done. I was taken aback by her question. I assumed everyone I met would know. I told her I was ready to deliver twin baby boys. She grinned behind her mask. She told me it was hospital policy to ask each patient what procedure they were scheduled for, as an effort to avoid mistakes. I told her I was going to have bone-graft surgery to both legs.

She then wheeled me into the operating room. As usual, the room was bitter cold. Surgical suites are kept cold so germs won't survive, not to keep doctors awake. I would have asked the nurse that question then but it was hard to talk. There was oldies-type rock-n-roll music playing loudly from a stereo system in the corner of the operating room. Six people dressed in surgical scrubs worked diligently with different pieces of surgical equipment in preparation for my operation. I noticed, hanging on one wall next to the stainless-steel operating table, a box with lights displaying my Xrays. I could see the massive breaks in my shin bones. Doctor Siek then came into the room. He was wearing the same drab green surgical scrubs as the other doctors except for one difference: His surgical mask and hat featured a bright-colored, flower print design. He walked over to me and asked if I was doing okay. He asked if I had any questions before I went to sleep. I asked if he could make me six feet four inches tall! He asked me why I wanted to be so tall. I told him I always wanted to play in the NBA. Then the anesthesiologist told me to count from ten backwards. I reached the number seven before the light went out.

Three weeks following the surgery, I was discharged from the hospital and transported back to the nursing home. My workman's compensation insurance carrier refused to hold my room at the nursing home so I had to share a room until another private room opened up.

I shared a room with a man in his sixties who had apparently suffered a stroke. He was paralyzed on one side of his body and confined to a wheelchair. He would push himself around with his one good arm and leg. His words were terribly slurred because of the stroke, making him almost impossible to understand. Even though he had difficulty speaking, he had no trouble exercising his throat and lungs by snoring at night. I have never heard a human snore as loud as this man! He would retire for the evening at about 7:30 P.M., so he was sawing logs by the time I tried to sleep. It became impossible for me to get to sleep. I was confined to my bed at the nursing home, still weak from major surgery, so I would try to sleep when my roommate would go off to lunch or dinner. That was difficult during the day with all the noise coming from the hall and the intercom system constantly paging people. I was not getting the sleep I needed to recover from surgery. I was losing weight at an alarming rate, my facial color had turned ashen, and I was becoming quite withdrawn. The staff did not have a place to relocate my roommate, so at night, nurses would unplug my bed and push it out into the hallway where I would sleep. Even though the nurses tried to be as quiet as possible, it was still difficult to get a good night's sleep. I was able to get a bit more sleep once I adjusted to the new sounds in the hallway. My color returned as well as my strength. I even started to regain my appetite. About two weeks after returning to the nursing home, a private room became available and I was moved. It was nice to have privacy back after using the bedpan in the hallway.

My doctor contacted a company called Electro-Biology Incorporated to fit me with a pair of Bilateral Electrical Stimulating Units. Their purpose was to run a small amount of electrical current through the area where my legs were broken. The current might stimulate the newly grafted bone to grow and become solid again. The difficult part of this treatment was that most patients who benefit from this procedure have only one leg or arm treated. Since I had both legs being treated at once, the pads used on each of my legs were interfering with each other. The technician from the company said this could cause more harm than good. To solve the problem, I had to keep 24 inches between my legs so the pads attached to my left leg would not interfere with pads attached to my right leg. My dad brought in a broom handle that he had cut to the required 24 inches. I was instructed to run the machines twelve hours a day, for one month. I chose to do it at night while I slept. So, each night after my dinner was served, I would place the broom handle between my legs to maintain the proper distance of 24 inches.

Within a few weeks of using these machines, the doctors determined that my shin bones were starting to produce new growth in the area of the breaks. I was starting to heal! For the first time since the crash, I was showing real signs of progress. I knew I had a long way to go, but nevertheless, I was healing. My spirits were raised.

TWENTY-THREE

The Magic Table

After my legs started to mend and my shin bones became solid, Dr. Siek wrote an order for me to start physical therapy on a special table. On this table, the patient is placed on his or her back. Straps are placed across the patient's body, starting from the middle of the chest down to the ankles. A therapist then slowly turns a wheel on the side of the table, which eventually brings the table to an upright position, allowing the patient to bear full weight on the legs. It may take several months of therapy to bring the patient and the table to a full upright position.

When the doctor told me about this table, I was excited about the prospect of bearing full weight on my legs. This was something my first doctors told me would be impossible. I knew this was my ticket home so I couldn't wait for the table to arrive. At eleven each morning, I would wheel myself down to the office and wait for deliveries to be made in anticipation of the incline table. For two weeks my routine was the same every morning. Every delivery man who walked in with packages was bombarded with questions. Most of them were so surprised to see a young man in my condition they didn't even hear my questions. Instead they asked me a thousand questions about what happened to me and why was I in a nursing home. For two weeks I waited, not patiently.

Then it happened! As I took my regular position, a UPS truck pulled up. This particular delivery man was earlier than most. He backed the truck up and as he opened the rear doors, I could see what looked like a large package with wheels. My heart was racing and the sight of that package brought tears to my eyes. I knew this was my table and it would allow me to eventually walk out of the nursing home and back into my life.

The delivery man pushed my table down to the other end of the nursing home. I was wheeling as fast as I could, trying to keep up with him. I explained how the table worked and how I would soon be leaving the nursing home. A short course of therapy on the incline table and I could go home, I told him.

I was no stranger to physical therapy at the nursing home. Even though I hadn't been given permission to participate, I would visit the therapist and ask questions about how to strengthen and stretch my muscles. I would do leg lifts and other exercises they explained to me. I hated sitting around waiting to heal and wanted to be proactive in the healing process. The therapists were patient, even in the beginning when I wasn't supposed to be doing any form of exercise. One of the physical therapists was later quoted in a newspaper article saying, "Since working with Mark, I've had to get in better shape to keep up with him."

The incline table was wheeled into the small physical therapy room. There were several elderly residents performing exercises from their wheelchairs. The head therapist, Pam, was working with an elderly man. I'm sure she saw the excitement in my face when I parked my wheelchair perpendicular to the table. I locked the wheels on my chair and eventually pulled myself from the wheelchair to the table. I did this so quickly and quietly Pam did not even notice.

As I sat on the table with my legs extended outward, I scooted down so the edges of my casts were flush against the metal foot platform. When Pam finished with her patient, I asked her to explain how the table worked. I remember a puzzled look on her face when she saw that I was now on top of the table. "I'll explain how the table works after you explain to me how you got from your wheelchair onto the table," she said. She told me how the table worked but reminded me that my therapy sessions were not supposed to start for another week. Pam also made it clear I would need to have patience because it would be several months before I could achieve full weight-bearing position.

I asked her how the straps worked as I attempted to fit myself onto the table. She helped by tightening the straps across my body until I was securely fastened in place. Then I asked how the wheel mechanism on the side of the table worked. She grew more nervous with my line of questioning. She told me she could get into trouble for even allowing me to be on the table. I assured her I was not in any discomfort and everything would be fine.

Next, I asked her to turn the wheel that elevated the table. I could sense Pam was getting irritated. "Absolutely not," she said. "Now let's get you off the table before I get in trouble!" But I wasn't ready to quit yet. I promised her that at the first sensation of pain or discomfort, I would get off the table. I convinced her to tilt the table to an upright position.

At first Pam turned the wheel only a quarter of a turn. I barely felt the table tilt. As she turned the wheel a little more, I could feel the table raise to an upright position. Pam constantly asked me if I felt any pain or discomfort. I assured her I was fine. I encouraged her to turn the wheel yet another turn. And again I was met with a resounding "No!" I pleaded with her, "Please, Pam, this is my ticket out of here. I promise, the slightest amount of discomfort and I will stop!" She eventually gave in to my requests.

Over the next forty minutes, I was raised to a full upright position. I was thrilled. Only a month had passed since my last surgery and here I was strapped to a table with my feet resting on a metal platform, bearing my full weight. I stayed in that position for about ten minutes. I felt somewhat dizzy, I also experienced a tingling sensation in my legs from the blood rushing down to my feet. This was the first time I had been in a complete upright position in a year. Pam didn't realize how tall *I* was; I didn't realize how short *she* was. Everybody looks like a giant to those of us in wheelchairs. I was excited about being in a normal position and looking Pam straight in the eyes. I had become accustomed to looking up at everyone, but now I was on her level and it felt great. Pam constantly asked me how I felt and if I was ready to be lowered back down. But I wanted to stay on the table. For the first time in my recovery, I could see a light at the end of my very long and dark tunnel. And finally it wasn't a train bearing down on me!

After thirty minutes of being upright, I became more light headed. I told Pam to begin to lower the table back to a horizontal position. As she did, I heard a cracking noise coming from the table. I started slipping toward the floor. The security straps were now positioned under my chin. "Are you okay?" Pam shrieked. The platform holding my feet came loose, dropped a couple inches, and then rested on the floor. The weight of my body, along with the weight of the casts on my legs, made it impossible for Pam to lower the table back to a horizontal position. I was stuck upright.

Pam was in a panic but I was laughing. "Mark, it's not funny! Stop laughing and do something. I could get fired for this!" she said. I reminded her I was the one strapped to the table like Frankenstein. There wasn't a lot I could do to help. I told Pam to push my wheelchair in front of the table and then undo the straps from across my body. I would simply, with her help, step off the metal platform and walk to my wheelchair. Pam was speechless and lost all the color in her face. I was about to take my first steps and I wasn't even supposed to be on the table for another week. I just accomplished something that was supposed to take several months. I figured I cut two months off my stay at the nursing home as I prepared to take my first steps since that Halloween night!

Pam told me to stay calm and not move. She was going to get help. She returned with an additional therapist. Together, they unstrapped me from the table and held me tightly on both sides. I took two steps toward my parked wheelchair and sat down. They asked if I felt discomfort in my legs. "No. Let's do that again. That was fun," I said with a grin. Pam did not think my comment was amusing. She immediately wheeled me back to my room and asked me if I felt any pain in my legs. I assured her I was fine. That day was the most successful day of my recovery. I took two steps! My first group of doctors told me that would be impossible. I love it when God proves people wrong!

Pam called Dr. Siek to tell him what happened. He drove to the nursing home immediately. When he arrived, he wanted to see for himself how I was able to stand without any discomfort. I took two or three steps as I held onto the walker with Pam and Doctor Siek holding my sides. Then I sat down in my wheelchair. My body was still weak from my experience with the incline table and I was exhausted after my short walk. Doctor Siek was excited but cautious. He told me to stop walking until Xrays could be taken to check my bones. He said if there was a suffi-cient amount of healing in my legs, he would replace the long leg casts with short leg casts so I could start work on bending my knees. Once I regained motion in my knees, I would be allowed to walk with a walker and my therapist nearby. I could taste freedom! I knew in my heart I would be going home soon.

TWENTY-FOUR

Short-Leg Casts

That next morning I was transported to Doctor
Siek's office. I prayed my legs would be healed
enough to use short-leg casts. I also thanked the Lord for
the opportunity to stand and walk in one day. I believe it
was nothing less than a miracle from God that allowed me
to stand and walk in such a short time after surgery. I
remember those who witnessed it saying things such as
"It's a modern day miracle!" and "God healed that young
man!"

The Xrays showed a remarkable amount of healing in
the month following the bone-graft surgery. I was fitted

with short-leg casts and special booties attached like shoes on the bottom of my casts so I could walk easier. The doctor wrote an order for manipulation of my knees to regain the movement I lost from being in the long-leg casts. He also sent word to the medical supply company to come pick up their incline table. I often wonder if they ever rented a table for such a short period of time.

The next few weeks were spent loosening the stiffness in my knees. The therapy was extremely painful but I knew I was on my way to recovery and my independent life. When the pain of bending and stretching my muscles would bring me to tears, I thought about the day I would walk back into the police department and resume my career. That thought helped ease the pain.

TWENTY-FIVE

Going Home

After a few weeks, I had an appointment for another series of Xrays. I was confident these Xrays would reveal large amounts of new bone growth. When the Xrays were developed, I was shown firsthand how the break areas were now almost solid with new bone growth. I was so excited!

My first question was, "Can I go home today?" Dr. Siek then said something I'd longed to hear over the past year and a half. "Yes, Mark, I think it will be okay if you go home!" Wow and double wow! I was going home! No more nursing home, no more institutional food. I was going home. I kept repeating it. I wanted someone to pinch me to make sure I wasn't dreaming. I was going home! I must have repeated it fifty times in the doctor's office. I didn't try to hide my tears. They were tears of joy, not disappointment. I couldn't care less if people saw a grown man crying like a baby. I was going home!

Back at the nursing home, I couldn't wait to tell the staff the good news. As excited as I was about leaving, I was also a little sad. For over a year, I had been cared for by the staff of Belleair East Nursing Home. They were such professionals and wonderful people. I had bonded with so many of them. When I announced the good news of my healing and pending departure, many tears were shed. The staff was excited about my returning home, but they, too, felt sad. I had become part of the family at the nursing home and to this day, I hold onto some wonderful memories from Belleair East Nursing Home.

TWENTY-SIX

Back Home, Back to Work

My legs became stronger each day as I walked the halls of my parents' condominium. I became a familiar sight, strolling along behind my walker. My legs finally regained some muscle definition, instead of looking like two sticks protruding from my shorts. The more I walked, the more definition returned. My leg muscles could never come close to the form they were before the crash. I had actually lost a great deal of my muscle but I was able to strengthen what I had remaining.

I soon advanced from a walker to crutches. From this point, I really took off. I could measure progress daily. I could put more and more weight on my legs. I became less dependent on my crutches although my knees and ankles were still tight and stiff. I had lost a great deal of movement in my joints due to being immobile for almost two years. My doctor was pleased with my progress and ordered specially fitted braces to be worn while walking. The braces were attached to specially made shoes that I was supposed to wear for several weeks until my legs gained enough strength to walk without the support of crutches.

After wearing the braces for only a couple days, I got an inclination to walk from one side of my room to another without them. I hated strapping the braces on every time I wanted to walk or go to the bathroom. I remember holding onto my bed and standing up. I was amazed and relieved: No pain or sounds of shattering bone! Then, while still tightly holding my bed, I took a small step with my right foot. I displaced all my weight onto my right foot and leg and noticed there was little discomfort. With each small step, I held onto the bed a little less. Before long, I was walking around my room without the support of braces or crutches. I could hear my mom and dad talking in the kitchen so I decided to surprise them with my new achievement. While holding my braces in one hand and my crutches in the other, I slowly made my way into the kitchen. The look on my parents' faces was amazing. "What in the world are you doing," my mother exclaimed. "You're going to hurt yourself." My dad thought I was pushing things a little to fast. Maybe so, but I now had the taste of total freedom. There was no turning back.

A few days later as my dad and I ate lunch at the kitchen table, I dropped a second bombshell in his lap. (The first was me walking into the kitchen holding my braces and crutches.) I wanted to try driving. Shocked, he asked if I was serious. "Yes," I explained. "I want to go for a drive." "Are you sure you are ready to do this?" my dad asked with a nervous twinge in his voice. "Of course I am! I feel great," He grabbed his wallet and the keys to my car. As I climbed into my car, it was as if I never stopped driving. The only adjustment I had to make was to move the seat forward a little. I had lost one even inch in both legs. I also had to adjust the radio back to my country music station. A flood of independence came back to me as I sat behind the wheel again.

My dad was quick to point out that I hadn't driven in quite some time and therefore, we should stay on the back streets until I polished my driving skills. I think he was more concerned about his welfare and public safety than he was about my confidence. As my dad and I pulled out of the parking lot, I could see my mother standing there shaking her head in disbelief. My dad and I drove around the neighborhood for about half an hour. It was as comfortable to me as if I had never stopped driving. I felt great! No one would have imagined me doing this two years ago. Now, here I was, driving like everyone else on the road.

As my dad sat in the passenger seat, he continually asked me, "Do you want me to take over from here?" I just kept smiling and driving. The one concern I had was whether I would be strong enough to apply the brake pedal if I needed to stop quickly. Once I proved to myself and my dad that I was capable of driving in all circumstances safely, I became a man on the go!

The next morning, I took my first solo drive to the police department. When I walked into the lobby without any casts or braces, and just crutches for stability, I surprised everyone. The secretaries saw me first. They congregated around me and bombarded me with questions about my recovery and prognosis. Many had tears in their eyes. They were genuinely concerned. The word spread quickly that I was there. Before long I was surrounded by not only secretaries but patrol officers, administrators, and detectives. Even some of the more hardened street cops were caught wiping away a tear or two. I was back!

I spent most of the morning walking around, catching up on news and war stories from my fellow officers. I realized how much I missed the officers and my job. I longed to be back in uniform, patrolling the streets. I also realized how fortunate I was to be working for a police department that cared. The Dunedin Police Department was not large, with approximately sixty to seventy officers, but it wasn't considered small, either. To me it was the perfect size! Everyone cared for everyone else.

I was soon back in Captain Sam Raney's office pleading with him to allow me to return to my job. He said I could return with my doctor's permission. So I called and scheduled an appointment with Doctor Siek. During the time I spent waiting for my appointment, I increased my physical endurance by exercising and walking twice a day.

Dr. Siek was not surprised with what I was trying to accomplish during rehabilitation, but he had my best interests at heart. He delayed my return to work for several weeks. During that time I would work even harder during my therapy sessions. I joined a spa and started lifting light weights with my legs. I quickly put away my crutches and walked on my own two legs. I started by walking slowly, calculating and concentrating on each and every step. By the end of the third week I was walking with confidence and ease. I set daily goals.

Each day as I awoke, I thanked God for healing me and giving me another day of life. I never forgot that if it weren't for the Lord, I would have been another DUI statistic. I knew where my drive and motivation came from. Through prayer, I drew my strength. The daily goals helped me stay focused on what I needed to accomplish.

I went back to Siek's office asking again to return to work. He agreed but with some stringent parameters. I was not allowed to work any patrol duties until further notice. I was only allowed to perform office work half days until he said otherwise. I was still excited about accomplishing my second goal. I was returning to work! The only goal I had yet to achieve was to run in a race, but at least I was finally returning to my childhood dream.

My doctor sent a letter to the police chief spelling out my limitations and the conditions of my return to law enforcement. Captain Raney contacted me regarding the doctor's letter and set a date that I was to officially report back to duty. I was instructed to report to the Detectives Division at 8:00 A.M. on June 1, 1983. Wow, I would be a detective! I was anxious to learn of my new duties.

The night before my return to work, I received several phone calls from the detectives, congratulating me. I was also made aware of a tradition within the division. The new man has to bring doughnuts for everyone! I was no exception. I was also told that the newspapers and TV stations had learned of my return and wanted to film a story. One of the local newspapers assigned a reporter to document my every move on the big day.

That night, I couldn't sleep. I was so excited about returning to the job I loved. I was also anxious about resuming my career. I must have asked myself a thousand questions. Was I physically ready? Would I be able to learn my new assignments as a rookie detective? Would the officers at the police department feel comfortable with my return? And of course, would I find a doughnut shop open at 7:00 A.M. on my way to work?

My alarm sounded at 6:00 A.M. I sprang to my feet. I had already laid out the suit I was to wear, along with freshly polished shoes. My mother and father were up and my mother was cooking breakfast. I was too excited to eat. My parents wished me well. I could sense the concern in my mother's voice. I know she had hoped I would take a new direction with my career once I had recovered, but both my parents supported my decision to return to police work.

My first stop that next morning was the local donut shop. I wasn't sure this so-called "tradition" about bringing doughnuts was true. I had a sneaky feeling this was a scam but, to make sure, I picked up two dozen doughnuts on my way in. I had been instructed to arrive as close to 8:00 A.M. as possible. This was to ensure that the local media would get pictures of my return. Sure enough, when I pulled into the parking lot, there were TV crews and newspaper reporters everywhere. I was greeted by reporters asking me questions all at once. I tried to answer as many as I could, but I began to wonder if I would ever make it into the building. I think every imaginable question was asked of me that morning. Several officers saw the predicament I was in and waded into the sea of reporters to rescue me.

The first to welcome me back was my friend and captain, Sam Raney. I found myself surrounded again but this time by coworkers and friends. It was a wonderful homecoming. The first day of work consisted of greeting all my friends, being assigned new equipment, and learning what assignments I would have as a new detective.

One reporter from a local newspaper followed me all day. I answered lots of questions and posed for many pictures. By the close of business, I was exhausted. My legs were swollen, my ankles were the size of grapefruits, but I felt great. After all, I was back at work!

Several weeks after settling in, I began to feel comfortable. I was back to a somewhat average work day. I wasn't looked upon by my colleagues as the injured officer fighting my way back. Instead, and thankfully so, I was just another detective.

One morning as I sat at my desk and reviewed police reports, someone delivered the mail. I was still getting letters and post cards wishing me well and congratulating me on my return to police work. This particular morning was no different in that I had several greeting cards in my stack of mail.

But I was surprised at the return address on one of the card-sized envelopes. It read simply, "The White House." I looked around the office, anticipating smiling faces or snickering. I knew this had to be another practical joke. Practical jokes are as common around any police department as are men and women in uniform. To my surprise, nobody was looking my direction and all the other detectives were busy at their desks.

I opened the envelope and pulled out a neatly folded letter. Centered at the top of the stationery was the presidential seal. I looked down toward the bottom of the letter for the name of the sender. There it was in dark black ink: Ronald Reagan! I looked around the room again in an attempt to catch someone hiding a smile or a laugh. Everyone was still busy with paperwork or mail. I looked back at the envelope to make sure I hadn't opened someone else's mail. It was addressed to me. After I read the letter, I held it in the air above my head and asked the other detectives if this was a joke.

They gathered around my desk to take turns reading the letter and studying the signature of the sender. They assured me this was no joke and the signature of Ronald Reagan appeared to be authentic. I was shocked. Why would the president of the United States write me? I'm an average guy, no one important. The president wrote me a letter and even said he and Nancy would be praying for me? Why?

The word soon spread that I had received a letter from the president. Many people stopped by to read the letter. I was moved and touched that the president of the greatest country in the world would take time to write me a letter. I've shared this letter with many people over the years and to this day it is proudly displayed in my office at home.

THE WHITE HOUSE
WASHINGTON

August 1, 1983

Dear Mr. Franzman:

I was sorry to hear that this has been a difficult two years for you. I know from my own life that the Lord never gives us a challenge without providing us with the strength to meet it. For the past two years you have been conquering great obstacles. I was pleased and proud to hear that you are back with the Dunedin Police Department. The dedication, courage, and love which have sustained and strengthened you are examples for us all.

Our nation owes a debt of gratitude to the men and women who, like you, place the safety and welfare of their fellowman before their own. You should take great pride in your accomplishments and your devotion to the Dunedin community.

Please know that Nancy and I will keep you in our thoughts and prayers. God bless you.

Sincerely,

Ronald Reagan

TWENTY-SEVEN

Retirement

Over the next year, I was able to return to full time employment with the city of Dunedin. I eventually returned to the patrol division as a patrol officer. However, I never was able to regain full motion in my knees and ankles. This proved to be a problem.

One evening, I was dispatched to an accident scene to assist with directing traffic on a two-lane country road. This crash happened on one side of a sharp curve. My assignment was to slow traffic speed so drivers wouldn't come upon the accident scene or emergency response personnel too quickly.

It was 6:00 P.M., just beginning to turn dark. I positioned my car on the side of the road, approximately 35
yards from the sharp curve.

The traffic in both directions approached and maneuvered around the accident scene as we had planned. There
was a break in the traffic for a minute, then a single car
approached in my direction. I could hear the engine of the
vehicle decelerating, just as the many other cars had done
past this accident. As the vehicle went by my patrol car,
some thirty yards in front of me, I gave the universal hand
signals to slow down. Instead of complying, as all the other
cars had done, this particular driver started to accelerate. I
couldn't believe my ears and eyes. I could hear the engine
gear up and see the car speed up.

I flashed the beam from my flashlight toward the driver
to get his attention. Instead, he kept accelerating. I thought
I was encountering a drunk driver again. I felt my heart
pounding as if it would explode through my chest. I radioed
to the officers that were on the other side of the curve that
a vehicle was approaching and refusing to slow down.

By this time, I made the decision to abandon my post
and run out of the way of the oncoming vehicle. I had not
yet regained full use of my legs and was unable to run with
any speed. As fast as this car was moving and as slow as I
was in running, I knew I was going to be struck again. All
I could do was position myself to try to jump on the hood
of the approaching car instead of being sucked under it. I
knew I stood a better chance of survival this way.

The driver of the approaching vehicle slammed the
brakes so hard that they locked. This caused the car to skid

violently and it finally came to a stop just a few feet away from me. I could see white smoke from the overheated tires and brakes. The smell of burning rubber filled my lungs and caused me to gasp for breath.

Several officers ran over to me after hearing the screech-ing of tires. Two other officers approached the driver, who was still sitting in a frozen state behind the steering wheel of his car. The officers pulled him out of the suspect car and expected to encounter another drunk driver.

This case proved to be different. This driver was not drunk. He was a young man who had just received his driver's license that day. He could clearly see me standing in the roadway giving him hand signals but thought I was motioning for him to speed up. He said he was nervous about driving by himself for the first time and was con-fused about what he was supposed to do so he panicked. We gave him a warning and sent him home.

However, I learned something important that evening. I knew I was potentially putting other officers' lives at risk by not being able to run very quickly. On October 24, 1985, I did the most difficult thing I have ever had to do: I retired from the Dunedin Police Department. I was able to stay on as a reserve officer and offer my services as needed. I couldn't just walk away. I had to stay involved in law enforcement in some capacity.

I have had the privilege of working with many dif-ferent divisions within the police department as a reserve officer. I was able to work with the patrol division during special events such as parades and high school football games. I worked in the detective, vice and narcotics; and marine divisions, as well as the crime prevention unit. I had a great career.

In 1995 the citizens of the city of Dunedin chose to dissolve the hundred-year-old police department in an effort to lower taxes. The local sheriff's department assumed law enforcement duties for the city. In 1995 I said a final good-bye to sixteen years of service to the Dunedin Police Department.

TWENTY-EIGHT

A New Direction

One of the most rewarding assignments I have had as a police officer has been crime prevention. Through this area of law enforcement, I have had many opportunities to share my story of how I overcame hurdles and adversity. In crime prevention my duties included school presentations, law enforcement exhibits at area malls, and attending job fairs as a recruiter. This provided me numerous audiences to hear about the dangers of drunk driving, the importance of setting goals, and how to overcome adversities.

Shortly after returning to work in 1983, I was also asked to share my story with members of my church. I spoke from my heart, sharing how I felt that my healing was a miracle from God. I shared with the congregation how I would pray before each surgery, and at the beginning of each day, for strength to continue. I told them I believed God was in the miracle-working business. I shared my simple story of how God healed me. My life was changed forever that Sunday morning when I spoke to the people I had worshipped with for six years.

Many audience members came up to me after the service to tell me how my story had touched their hearts and helped them. Many told me that by hearing my story, they were motivated as never before to continue fighting their own personal battles. Some told me how they were thinking of quitting before coming to that service, but now they were leaving church with a renewed strength to keep fighting. One lady told me I may have very well saved her life. She was dealing with an addiction and had tried many times to bring it under control. Although she had recently thought about suicide, she now had a new desire to overcome her addiction.

That night in bed, I thought about the service and all the people who told me my story helped them. The Lord reminded me of a verse of Scripture. It was written in the front of the book on angels that had been mysteriously placed in the intensive care unit next to my bed. That book was the first thing I saw when I awoke from my first surgery. I got out of bed and found the book.

When He heard this, Jesus said, "This sickness
will not end in death. No, it is for God's Glory
so that God's Son may be glorified through it.
                                        John 11:4

At that moment, I decided to tell my story to as many
people as would listen. Since the crash, I have had the privilege of speaking to thousands of people on the subject of
overcoming adversity, setting goals and forgiving others. I
have addressed people at churches, schools, corporations,
civic groups, prison youth camps, and Sunday school
classes. I feel that I am a blessed and privileged man to
have such a life-changing story to share all over the
country. By writing this book, I have one more avenue to
reach people who are hurting and struggling with personal adversity.

Overcoming
Adversity

TWENTY-NINE

Defining Adversity

There are many books on the subject of how to deal with adversity. I include this topic to offer practical advice on how to overcome your own adversity. I did much research on this topic by reading books and searching the Internet. I've incorporated my own thoughts on surviving the difficult times in our life. I don't consider myself an expert, but I have survived a great deal of adversity and beaten the odds by walking on my own again. I feel it is important to share with you my views on how to overcome your personal battles.

Adversity! What is it? The Merriam-Webster dictionary defines adversity as "hard times, misfortune." The American Heritage dictionary defines adversity as "great hardship, misfortune, calamitous event. A disaster, great distress."

There is no escaping it. We all face adversity. There are going to be hard times and tribulations in our lives. Regardless of our relationship with God, we all face our share of adversity. But thanks to God's grace, we can survive these hard times and even grow in our faith during difficult times.God's word makes it very clear to us that we will face adversity:

> *In fact, everyone who wants to live a Godly life*
> *in Christ Jesus will be persecuted.*
> 2 Timothy 3:12 (NIV)

The adversity that we face may come in the form of personal tragedy:

- The doctors say, "It's cancer."
- A loved one suffers the effects of multiple sclerosis.
- Alzheimer's disease steals the mind of someone you love.
- A stroke takes away your freedom.
- Parkinson's disease causes you to lose control of your body.
- A child is born dead or dies young.
- An accident leaves you disabled.

- A drunk driver kills a family member.
- A hurricane, flood, tornado, or fire destroys your home and possessions.
- You've been laid off or fired from your job.

Christians often feel that because they have made a commitment to Christ, they will be protected by God from experiencing terrible and tragic events in their life. This type of thinking causes these believers to be caught off guard. Adversity may shake and chip away at their foundation of their faith. They do themselves a great injustice believing they will live an adversity-free life when they become Christians.

Instead of being naïve, we should prepare ourselves for difficult times. We all are going to face adversity. The trials of life are going to come. Life can be very difficult! No where in the Bible does it say that God is going to keep Christians free of adversity or allow adversity to affect only those who may deserve it most. We all know people who are dishonest and full of themselves who seem to coast through life untouched, catching all the breaks. On the other hand, we may know someone who is always helping others and sincere in friendships. That person may seem to have a dark cloud above and never catch a break. Life is not always fair.

Having a belief that trouble *will* come is not necessarily pessimistic. Rather, it's a realistic attitude which prepares us to seek God's face even during the most difficult of times. Every person knows of someone who has successfully dealt with adversity in their life, someone who not only moved through it, but moved beyond it in faith and courage. We all know of persons who, when they experienced difficult and adverse conditions, displayed incredible strength and courage. Adversity is essential in growing in faith. I don't know anyone who has experienced any significant growing in faith without adversity. During adversity, we are pulled and stretched… we feel uncomfortable. We wonder what is going to happen next. We feel like we are coming apart at our seams. We wonder how on earth we will survive this storm. Adversity will test us and challenge us.

Through adversity we learn who we really are and what we are made of when we face hard times. God has a way of polishing, molding, and shaping us into the kind of people He wants us to become through the power of His love and grace. There is always a reason why we go through adversity! I think it's best explained in the book of 2 Corinthians:

> *To keep me from becoming conceited because of these surpassingly great revelations, there was given me a thorn in my flesh, a messenger of Satan, to torment me. Three times I pleaded with the Lord to take it away from me. But he said to me "My Grace is sufficient for you, for my power is made perfect in weakness." Therefore I will boast all the more gladly about my weaknesses, so that Christ's power may rest on me. That is why, for Christ sake, I delight in weaknesses, in insults,*

in hardships, in persecutions, in difficulties. For
when I am weak, then I am strong.

2 Corinthians 12:7-10 (NIV)

In this scripture from the Bible, the apostle Paul tells us he pleaded with God through prayer and fasting on three separate occasions to remove the thorns. But God allowed it to remain. The Lord never allows anything to touch our lives outside of His perfect will, so we can be assured that any suffering or hurt has a purpose. I think the ultimate goal of adversity is to strengthen our trust and our personal relationship with God. When we go to God in prayer for help, He promises not only to become our strength, but also to give us peace. The Bible is clear about the adversity and suffering we all endure at times and how God will see us through those difficult times:

We do not want you to be uniformed, brothers,
about the hardships we suffered in the Province
of Asia. We were under great pressure, far
beyond our ability to endure, so that we
despaired even of life. Indeed, in our hearts we
felt the sentence of death. But this happened
that we might not rely on ourselves but on God
who raises the dead. He has delivered us from
such a deadly peril, and he will deliver us. On
him we have set our hope that he will continue
to deliver us, as you help us by your prayers.

2 Corinthians 1:8-11 (NIV)

THIRTY

Our Response to Adversity

Adversity affects the educated and illiterate, rich or poor, famous or unknown. Adversity is an equal opportunity attacker. We all struggle with adversity. At times, the difficulties we face seem to be more than we can handle. For some, the heartache and even physical pain can become so intense that faith in God may be weakened.

For others, the adversity they face only strengthens their personal relationship with God. I've learned that how we respond to adversity often reflects what type of relationship we have with God. There will be times God will clearly reveal to us why we faced a particular trial in our life. Often times, we will not receive a quick answer as to why we faced a particular trial. But asking God why we are facing an adverse time in our life is only normal. There is nothing wrong in asking why. Even Christ, when He was dying on the cross, asked "why?"

> *About the ninth hour Jesus cried out in a loud voice "My God, my God, why have you forsaken Me?"*
>
> Matthew 27:46 (NIV)

Feeling pain from many devastating injuries and hearing doctors say I would never walk on my own again was almost unbearable for me. I would often ask God why? Why did this happen to me? I'm one of the good guys. I'm the guy who dedicated his life to putting bad guys in jail to protect society. Why didn't this happen to one of the bad guys? Why didn't the drunk driver get hurt instead of me? And why did both of my legs have to be broken instead of just one?

When I asked God "why?" I didn't ask just once. Everyday I would ask that same question: "Why me, Lord?" I kept praying and sought His will during the turbulent times. Often God is preparing us, so that we may be able to accept and understand His reasons for allowing the adversity.

Adversity may be the result of disobedience or sin in our lives. If this is the case, then we only have ourselves to blame. God tells us there are going to be consequences to disobedience. So why blame God? Instead, we should confess our sins and then correct the wrong in our lives. God will forgive us if we are serious about turning away from sin in our lives. There is nothing you have done or are doing that God won't or can't forgive. We've all made mistakes. Just pray and ask God's forgiveness. Turn the page in your life and go on.

Sometimes adversity is from the devil himself. If you live for Christ, you will be attacked spiritually by the enemy. If the devil never seems to mess with you, then perhaps you should take a hard look at your spiritual walk. If you are living as God would have you live, the devil will be threatened and will do whatever he can to disrupt your service to the Lord. If you find that the devil is not bothering you much, maybe your walk with the Lord is so weak and non-threatening that the devil doesn't think you can do much to interfere with his game plan. If Satan chooses to attack you, he does not have free rein to do so. If we can learn to seek God's face during the storms in our life, God will help us grow. It was once said that the key to adversity is our response to it!

The Bible tells us in the book of Job that the devil had to seek permission from God to attack Job. When the devil causes temptation in our lives, this may be the reason for our adversity as well. God always puts limitations on the type and amount of temptation or adversity that we face.

One of the hardest things for me to do has been to leave my hurts and adversity with God. I often want to take them back and see if I can handle my problems by myself. This only causes me to become more frustrated and upset. God will always give me the strength to face my trials and tribulations. We all need to call out to God when we face adversity and ask Him to give us the right attitudes for that trial. Remember, there is a perfect plan designed by God for us behind all of our trials. If we are willing to submit completely to God during our adversity, then God is able to accomplish His perfect plan for our lives. This is a lesson I learned during my many trials.

THIRTY-ONE

Spiritual Growth in Adversity

Growth comes not so much on the mountain tops, but while we are in the valleys. It's so easy to feel that God is great and kind and loving when we are not dealing with adversity. When the trials hit, how does our image of God change? Is He still loving and kind and merciful or do we now have a different viewpoint of God? Adversity will always show us just what type of relationship we have with God. Think back now on the last time you found yourself in the midst of the storm. What was your response to God? Our view of God may change with each new adverse situation. But God never changes.

The Bible tells us in the book of Hebrews, "Jesus Christ is the same yesterday and today and forever." God's plan for our lives is not to see us defeated, nor to harm us. He wants us to have a great and prosperous future.

*For I know the plans I have for you, declares the
Lord, plans to prosper you and not to harm
you, plans to give you hope and a future.*
Jeremiah 29:11 (NIV)

Adversity can shake our self-esteem and create doubts about our own self-worth. I found myself on more than one occasion lying in my hospital bed asking, "Lord, what have I done to deserve this?" Or, "Why me Lord?" I think it's important to see the difference here in asking, "Why Lord?" and asking, "Why me Lord?" When we start asking, "Why *me*, Lord," this is self pity. Instead, try to determine what God may want to teach through the adversity. How does God view you?

*But you are a chosen people, a royal priesthood,
a holy nation, a people belonging to God, that
you may declare the praises of him who called
you out of darkness into his wonderful light.*
1 Peter 2:9 (NIV)

Adversity will shed light on our weaknesses as well as our strengths. Some people are destroyed by adversity. Others plow through the adversity and become stronger. Those folks never question whether they can make it through the storm. They just keep fighting until they have conquered their adversity.

With adversity comes the testing of our ability to forgive. Often our adversity is caused by the bad decisions of others. Maybe someone in your life has hurt you physically or emotionally. Those hurts can eat away at you for years or even a lifetime. It's important to reach a point in the healing process where you can forgive someone who has caused the hurt. This will help you grow and heal.

Adversity helps us measure our level of faith! When we are in the midst of storms, our true colors will shine bright. Sometimes those colors paint an embarrassing portrait of who we are. It's easy to pretend we are full of faith and confidence in God. But when dark clouds of adversity start to accumulate and the winds of adversity pick up, we may start to doubt God's ability to see us through the storm. Even Christ's disciples experienced doubt when they were caught at sea in a violent storm. But God always came through for them and He will for you, too.

When God delivers us from adversity, do we thank Him for His faithfulness? We should! Today I still thank God for the healing He has performed in my life. Not one of us can possibly know our own physical and emotional limits when it comes to adversity. However, God knows! As I was rushed into the emergency room, I was pleading for someone to kill me. I didn't think I could endure another second of pain. My remedy was death. But God's choice for me was life. God knew my limits even though I did not.

If you feel the storm you are facing is too much to handle and you see no way out, remember God put limits on all adversity! Because you are a child of God, He knows how much you can bear! God never makes mistakes!

A righteous man may have many troubles, but the Lord delivers him from them all.

Psalms 34:19 (NIV)

As a father has compassion on his children, so the Lord has compassion on those who fear him; for he knows how we are formed, he remembers that we are dust.

Psalms 103:13-14 (NIV)

Always remember no matter how bad the storm is right now, God loves you! You never have to go through the storm alone. God has not forgotten you!

See, I have engraved you on the palms of my hands; your walls are ever before me.

Isaiah 49:16 (NIV)

Don't let your adversity end in defeat. Instead, let it be the beginning of new growth and new maturity in your life and relationship with God.

Forgiveness
in Tragedy

THIRTY-TWO

Learning to Forgive

I have had the privilege of sharing my story with many different audiences. In speaking with audience members, I've discovered that one thing we all have in common is pain caused by others. We all harbor hurt, bad memories, and mental or even physical scars from those hurtful experiences.

Our minds work in incredible ways. We can hold onto and recall hurts, cutting words, and wrongs that have been inflicted upon us by friends or loved ones. Often painful memories are from years gone by, but are recalled as if they happened yesterday. Holding onto those awful memories may change us into hateful, angry and bitter people. Hurtful feelings can eat away at us if we hold them inside. Some spend their lives reliving painful memories, growing angrier each day. How do we deal with those scars and pains? How do we cleanse our minds from the hurts we have experienced from others? It comes down to one word—forgiveness!

The Bible has a lot to say about forgiveness:

> *For if you forgive men when they sin against you, your heavenly Father will also forgive you. But if you do not forgive men their sins, your Father will not forgive your sins.*
>
> Matthew 6:14-15 (NIV)

> *And when you stand praying, if you hold any-thing against anyone, forgive him, so that your Father in heaven may forgive you your sins.*
>
> Mark 11:25-26 (NIV)

> *Do not judge, and you will not be judged. Do not condemn, and you will not be condemned. Forgive, and you will be forgiven.*
>
> Luke 6:37 (NIV)

What is forgiveness? Forgiveness is a choice to release someone from what we believe he or she owes us. Forgiveness is an act of will, a choice by those who have been hurt by someone. It doesn't mean we will forget the wrong committed against us. Nor does it mean the hurt

Dead But Not Buried

wasn't real. Forgiveness means that we have chosen to free the offender from what we believe they owe us.

Forgiveness involves three elements: a wrong committed, a debt that is a result of that wrong, and the cancellation of that debt. All three elements are essential if forgiveness is going to take place. You may be saying, *Oh, but Mark you don't know how I've been hurt! You don't know what terrible things this person has done to me. There's no way I can forgive!*

God never said it would be easy to forgive, but He makes it clear that we must forgive. Being bitter does not ease pain! No matter how much bitterness we hold, it will never change the wrong done against us or undo the past. Bitterness has grave physical, emotional, and spiritual consequences. The individual who cannot forgive is always the loser. By not forgiving, we are forced to walk in the flesh rather than by the Spirit.

Think about your own situation, the wrong that was done against you! When the wrong was done, did you feel like developing a close friendship and becoming close friends with the offender? Or did you feel like striking back? Did you show gentleness in your actions toward that person or did you feel like blasting them with both barrels? Did you feel like giving in and accepting the wrong done against you or did you feel like fighting back? Most often we feel like blasting, retaliating, or physically fighting back. These are normal responses to being hurt. So what type of spirit should we have when dealing with our hurts. The Bible tells us in the book of Galatians what our spirit should produce when dealing with our hurts:

> *But the fruit of the Spirit is love, joy, peace,*
> *patience, kindness, goodness, faithfulness, gen-*
> *tleness, self-control; Against such things there is*
> *no law...Since we live by the Spirit, let us keep*
> *in step with the Spirit.*
>
> Galatians 5:22-23, 25 (NIV)

When we have an unforgiving spirit, we are prevented from walking in the Spirit. If we deal with our hurts on our own, we will likely fail! The only way I had victory and healing over my hurts was to surrender them to God. We need to be honest with God! He already knows how difficult it can be for us to forgive those who have hurt us. God will give us the wisdom and the strength to overcome hurt, anger, and pain. We just have to ask and believe.

> *But the wisdom that comes from heaven is first*
> *of all pure; then peace-loving, considerate, sub-*
> *missive, full of mercy and good fruit, impartial*
> *and sincere.*
>
> James 3:17 (NIV)

What are our options in overcoming hurt and disappointments? We have four options: First is to act as if nothing has happened. Second, we can strike back and try and even the score. The third is to forgive those who have hurt us, and the fourth option is to try and feel as others feel. So, let's take a closer look at each of our four options. First, we can hold the pain in and act as if nothing happened. By doing this, though, we may become bitter and angry and that will affect our physical and spiritual well-being. The anger and bitterness will eat away at us and will eventually affect our relationships and possibly every aspect of our lives. It may well destroy us!

When we have been hurt, we should deal with the hurt immediately. Don't let hurt fester and grow into something ugly and damaging. "Emotion follows motion. Forgiveness is first granted, then felt," someone once said. The fact that the Lord commands us to forgive indicates that we must obey Him and trust that the feelings will follow. Let the hurt go. Deal with it at once. In the book of Ephesians we are told how to handle our anger towards those who have wronged us:

> *In your anger do not sin. Do not let the sun go*
> *down while you are still angry.*
>
> Ephesians 4:26 (NIV)

Second, we can strike back at the one who has hurt us. We can try to even the score. If revenge is what we want, we can waste a great portion of our lives trying to get it. We can slander the offender or we can disrupt someone's business or personal life, all for the cause of getting even. As a police officer for over twenty years, I can attest to the extent to which some people cause physical injury and even death to those who have hurt them.

We need to turn our anger and feelings of "settling the score" over to the Lord. Let God "even the score" for you. Let God right the wrong. God has the wisdom to take our hurt and set us free from the desire to get even.

Do not take revenge, my friends, but leave room for God's wrath, for it is written: It is mine to avenge; I will repay, says the Lord.

Romans 12:19 (NIV)

We often think holding a grudge against those who have hurt us will somehow make them unhappy. Actually, the offender couldn't care less about what they have done to us or how we feel about them. It is God's business. He judges and punishes for wrongs. He doesn't need our help, advice, or interference. Three quotes about grudges that I refer to are these: William H. Walton said, "To carry a grudge is like being stung to death by one bee." Winston Churchill said, "Nothing is more costly, nothing is more sterile, than vengeance." Lord Kames said about forgiveness, "No man ever did a designed injury to another, but at the same time he did a greater to himself." And the Bible offers this:

Do not be overcome by evil, but overcome evil with good.

Romans 12:21 (NIV)

The third thing we can do is to forgive those who have hurt us. The Bible tells us in the book of Mark how we are to forgive:

And when you stand praying, if you hold anything against anyone, forgive him, so that your Father in heaven may forgive you your sins.

Mark 11:25 (NIV)

Finally, the fourth thing we can do—we can try to feel as others feel! If we are to forgive, we must learn to empathize with others. We must climb into their situation and try to feel as they feel. We must walk in their shoes. It's easy to stand back and pass judgment concerning someone's situation. It's also easy to tell someone else what they need to do, but empathy helps us avoid this mistake. We cannot experience everything life deals out and thankfully so. But we can make an honest attempt to consider what it would be like if we were in the situation facing another.

How does it feel to be handicapped, unable to walk, drive, or care for yourself? How does it feel to have such devastating injuries that you wake up and go to bed in pain? How does it feel to be unemployed with bills you cannot pay and children you cannot feed?

How does it feel to be a minority, living in a community where you are looked down on by others? How does it feel to be divorced, struggling through the pain of having the one you love leave you? How does it feel to be widowed or to lose a child or parent? How do you suppose it would feel to have cancer, Alzheimer's disease, or AIDS?

How do you think it would feel to be depressed, full of hopelessness, and not know why? How would it feel to be alone and unloved? How would it feel to be full of doubt and fear?

We can climb into someone else's situation, at least mentally, and walk a mile or two in their shoes. Once we do, we might find it easier to show tenderhearted love and genuine forgiveness. When we feel as they feel, we might understand why they act and react as they do. The greatest act of forgiveness ever displayed was that of Jesus Christ. He was falsely accused by wicked men. They unfairly convicted Him. They tortured Him, mocked Him, nailed Him to the cross and hanged Him until He died. As blood flowed from His head to His feet with His back ripped open from beatings, He looked down from the cross at those who did this to Him and prayed.

> *Jesus said, Father, forgive them, for they do not know what they are doing.*
>
> Luke 23:34 (NIV)

There was no bitterness in that prayer, only love and forgiveness.

Who do you need to forgive? What hurts do you need to turn over to the Lord? What bitterness and anger do you need to get rid of? Who do you need to apologize to for the way you have been treating them? Let me encourage you to set things right today. Don't put it off one more day. Ask God for help. Forgiveness is a promise that you can make and keep, whether you "feel like it" or not. I find it easier to forgive others when I remember Christ's great sacrifice.

Max Lucado in his book *He Still Moves Stones*, expressed these thoughts on forgiveness:

Bitterness Is Its Own Prison
The sides are slippery with resentment. A floor of muddy anger stills the feet. The stench of

betrayal fills the air and stings the eyes. A cloud of self-pity blocks the view of the tiny exit above. Stop in and look at the prisoners, victims of abuse. The dungeon, deep and dark, is beckoning you to enter. You can, you know. You've experienced enough hurt. You can choose, like many, to chain yourself to your hurt, or you can choose, like some, to put away your hurts before they become hates. How does God deal with your bitter heart? He promises you that what you have is more important than what you don't have. You still have your relationship with God. No one can take that.

THIRTY-THREE

The Race

In 1992, I heard about a race being held in Dunedin at midnight on the Fourth of July. One of the goals I had set was to run in a race someday. When I read about this race, it reminded me that the only goal I had yet to achieve was to run in a race.

I contacted the organization sponsoring the race and was told they were going to have two races on the Fourth of July. The first was a 3K (1.8 mile) run and the second a 10K (6.2 mile) run. I asked them to send me an entry form for the short race. When I provided my name and address, the person on the phone recognized my name. He wanted to know if I was the police officer who had been run over by a drunk driver on Halloween night. I told him I had been and he laughed. He then said I would not be able to participate in the race. I couldn't believe what I was hearing. I told him that I had set a goal to run in a race. Why wasn't I allowed to participate? The gentleman said, "I'm sorry, Mark. We don't have a wheelchair division." I assured him I was not riding but had every intention of running. My goal was to run 1.8 miles without walking. I set this goal to see if I could do it. And I did! It took me twenty-five minutes to complete the race. I ran the entire distance without walking.

But something far greater happened to me than accomplishing that goal. I received letters from many people who read about the race in the newspaper. People went on to say that after reading about how I overcame my adversities, their adversity no longer seemed so overwhelming. They planned to set their own goals and keep fighting. I was touched and moved by what I read in those many letters. I was amazed that running 1.8 miles helped so many people I didn't even know existed on this planet. How many more people could I inspire if I ran the 10K race the next year?

I set another goal! I vowed to run in the 10K race the following Fourth of July. I had to get back in the gym to strengthen my legs. After work, I would come home and run throughout my neighborhood, trying to increase my endurance. It took me a year to prepare. This time my motives were not based on selfish hopes but on inspiring others.

When the day arrived, there were more than a thousand runners registered for the 10K race. Race officials assigned the number "one" to me. I've been told that usually, the number "one" is reserved for the winner of the race from the previous year. Race officials thought it would be a nice gesture to allow me to wear that special number. Along with national media being present, Mothers Against Drunk Driving members were there in force. Several of the members made signs with wonderful words of encouragement for me. They positioned themselves along the course, and as I ran by, they held up their signs to cheer me on. I was moved by their support as well as the many other citizens who cheered me on. They inspired me to finish that race.

I was allowed to place myself at the front row so I could get the best start possible. From that vantage point, I saw 999 serious runners standing behind me! I had visions of becoming a human doormat, being so trampled I would be crippled and need to drink all my meals from a straw. Minutes before the race, I moved all the way to the rear of the pack. Out of a thousand racers, I started dead last. I wasn't there to beat anybody. Since it was a midnight race, I would have been content to finish sometime before the sun came up.

I completed the race an hour and twenty-five minutes later. But most important, I did not walk. I *ran* the entire 10K. I received letters from all over the country due to the national exposure. People who wrote to me told me how I had inspired them to overcome their own problems. They, too, were now setting goals.

THIRTY-FOUR

What's Next

Since retiring from the Dunedin Police Department on October 24, 1985, I have undergone many more operations, bringing my total to almost thirty. The most recent operation was in 1999. I developed traumatic arthritis in both my ankles and feet. It became too painful to walk for any length and time, so my doctors sent me back into the operating room and fused my left ankle. They placed two large screws through the ankle joint. I no longer have movement in my left ankle but this is the only way to alleviate pain. I've had to learn to walk without ankle movement.

On the positive side, I have had the privilege of traveling and sharing my incredible story with many different organizations. On one occasion, I shared my story with juvenile inmates at our local sheriff's boot camp facility. The letters I receive from these hurting kids is proof that this story changes lives. I have also created a Web site by which I can reach people all over the world.

If there are heroes in this story, they are my parents, Fred and Betty Franzman. I was not married at the time of the crash or during rehabilitation. My parents were with me every day to give me support and encouragement. I'm convinced they felt every pain I felt. Often, they would stop by my favorite restaurants and bring me a meal of real food. My parents sacrificed a lot, both as I was growing up and while I was recovering in the hospital and nursing home. I could not have been born to a more wonderful and supportive set of parents. Unfortunately, my father died due to complications of Alzheimer's disease in 2001.

My wife Linda has been through many of my operations with me. I met her at church in 1994 and we married in 1996. When she agreed to marry me, she knew the road would be rough at times. Linda has always been there to lift my spirits and encourage me to keep fighting. I would not have made it if it weren't for her. Linda is a devoted wife and mother, as well as a godly lady. When Linda gets on her knees to pray, I'm convinced all Heaven stops to listen. She is also a heroine in my story and the answer to many prayers. I was doubly blessed when God brought Linda to me. Not only did I marry a beautiful, intelligent, and compassionate wife, but my in-laws, are a blessing as well. Linda's parents, Bob and Jeanne Rice, and her brothers and sisters, Bob Rice, Tyler

Rice, Cindy Rice, Kathie Rice, and Sandra Hancock and their spouses and children are a blessing as well. I could not have married into a more loving and supportive family.

Our daughter Alexandria is thirteen years old and an intelligent and beautiful young lady, like her mom. Linda and I are blessed and proud to have such a talented and intelligent daughter. We know she will be a success at whatever she does.

My sister, Cheri Shelnutt, was living in Washington State during the time of my crash and recovery. I know she bathed me in prayer during this time, and for that I am forever grateful. She is now married to a wonderful and caring man named Jerry. They have four wonderful boys whose names are Joshua, Jeremy, Josiah, and Elijah. They reside on their Sweet Hollow Farm (sweethollowfarm@earthlink.net) in Bulls Gap, Tennessee, and are growing some of the finest organic produce in the state.

As I write this, Linda and I are in the process of adopting a daughter from China. We should have our little blessing in 2002. It will have taken us over a year to go through the adoption process. We have decided to name her Makayla.

Makayla is a special gift to us from God. I know in my heart she will touch many hearts and change many lives for the Lord in her lifetime. God has been so good to us! I am truly a blessed man!

I'd like to give credit to Dr. Gerard Siek, MD, the surgeon who had the vision and surgical skills that enabled me to walk again. I have the utmost respect for Dr. Siek as a physician and a surgeon. He truly is a gifted doctor.

After Dr. Siek retired, Dr. Thomas Schwab, MD, of Clearwater took over my care. He has performed many surgical procedures, and continues to advise me on my medical needs.

Dr. Schwab and his staff at the Orthopaedic Associates of West Florida are the most talented group of professionals in the state of Florida, if not the country. His expertise has played a key roll in my recovery and my continued ability to walk on my own two legs. To him I owe many thanks.

My prayer for you is that this story has touched your heart and encouraged you to overcome *your* adversity. If this story helps one person to find victory over personal struggle, I count this project a success. Please use this book over and over again with each new struggle and challenge you may face. Use it as a guide to help you, a loved one, or a friend through life's challenges. Always remember: When life knocks you on your back, never give up. As long as you keep getting back up, you are a winner! And remember this quotation that helped me during my difficult times:

"The truest measure of God's love is that He loves without measure!"

Thank You!

Mark Franzman

If you would like to book Mark for a personal appearance at your church, business, or organization or purchase Mark's story on video or cassette tape, please visit his Web site at: www.franzman.com

You may also write to Mark at the following address:
Mark Franzman
P.O. Box 8358
Clearwater, Florida 33758

A PERSONAL NOTE FROM MARK

Thank you for your interest in my story. I hope it has inspired and encouraged you to set goals to overcome your own adversity.

When I decided to put my story on paper, I struggled with many decisions. Where to begin? How much do I share with the readers? I decided to speak from my heart and tell you how I survived. I hope you will record your own personal notes and outline your own personal blueprint for overcoming adversity in this book. Please refer back to the areas of the book that spoke directly to you.

I refer to the Bible throughout this book. I could not have made it without prayer and the reassurance I received from God's word. One of the many lessons I've learned is that God is in the prayer-answering business. I would encourage each of you to develop a personal relationship with God. We can all say we believe there is a "Higher Power" or there is the "Big Man" upstairs in control. But I'm talking about an intimate and personal relationship with the Creator of the heavens and of the earth. With this type of relationship, God will be more personal to you, as a friend and a Father. I achieved this type of relationship by praying and inviting Jesus into my life as my personal Lord and Savior. My life has never been the same. I know God will hear my prayers and that He cares about my concerns.

Before each of my operations, I asked God to give me the strength to make it through. God never let me down! I personally saw miracles unfold in my life during my long recovery. I drew my strength from God and His word. That is why I often return to the scriptures that have meant so much to me during my adverse times.

If you would like to know how to develop a personal relationship with Jesus, please read the final chapter in this book, "The Roman Journey." It is an exciting trip through the book of Romans that will inspire and give you hope. Not everyone will spend eternity in heaven. God makes it very clear what we must do to get into heaven. You can't earn your way. It is the free gift from God. This chapter explains how to get into heaven and have a personal relationship with Jesus. It is the most important chapter in this book. I hope you will read it.

The Roman Journey

The most important and rewarding thing I have done in my life has been to develop a personal and intimate relationship with Jesus. When I was first introduced to the Christian faith, I had a lot of questions. I was never one to jump into something without first taking a good look before making a decision.

I now have assurance of where I'll spend eternity when I die. For the first time in my life, I have seen my prayers answered and God working in my life. Before, I felt as if my prayers weren't traveling much past the ceiling of the room I was praying in. But now, after becoming a

Christian, I see God working in every area of my life. He truly loves me in spite of my many mistakes and failures.

The purpose of this chapter is to share with you my experience and to answer questions about inviting Jesus into your heart and becoming a Christian. Jesus will never force Himself on you. It has to be a decision you make freely to follow Him. There are consequences in not believing and following Jesus, but He still allows you to decide for yourself whether you are going to believe.

I will share with you the questions I had about why I should believe in Jesus and the answers I received to those questions. I invite you to think about the following pages, search your heart, and then make your decision. My prayer is that you will enter into the most exciting and rewarding relationship you could ever experience—a relationship with Jesus, God's Son.

One of the first questions I had was: Why do I have to personally invite Christ into my heart? I'm going to heaven if I live a good life, aren't I? I'm a good guy. I'm not a criminal, I pay my taxes fairly, I love my family, and I am a good provider for them. My neighbors and colleagues think I'm a nice guy. There are a lot of people worse than I am. God will allow me into heaven if I'm a good guy, won't He?

Well, that seems to make sense. But if we look at what God says about that, we will see that being a good person is not enough.

As it is written: There is no one righteous, not even one.

> *...for all have sinned and fall short of the glory of God.*
>
> Romans 3:10,23 (NIV)

The Bible says that we all have fallen short of what it takes to get into heaven. We are all sinners in God's eyes. I never would have considered myself a sinner, but God says we are all sinners. So, what must I do to get myself into heaven? What must happen? Let's look further in the book of Romans at how God takes care of our shortcomings.

> *You see, at just the right time, when we were still powerless, Christ died for the ungodly. Very rarely will anyone die for a righteous man, though for a good man someone might possibly dare to die. But God demonstrates His own love for us in this: While we were still sinners, Christ died for us.*
> *Since we have now been justified by His blood, how much more shall we be saved from God's wrath through Him!*
>
> Romans 5:6-9 (NIV)

My question about getting into heaven was answered by this scripture: I can do nothing! That's correct. There is nothing I can do on my own to get into heaven. I can't work harder, I can't try to be nicer to people. I can't give more money to charities or churches to assure my entrance into heaven. I can't earn my way into heaven. I'm truly powerless.

But God showed His love to us, even if we have failed miserably in our lives. God made a way for us to get into heaven. He sent His only begotten Son, Jesus, to die for us. Jesus took all of our wrongs and went to the cross and died, taking our punishment for us. By doing that, all of our past, present, and future sins are forgiven by God. God loves each of us so much He sent Jesus to His death so we might have life. What does this sacrifice mean to me? The book of Romans answers that question.

For the wages of sin is death, but the gift of God is eternal life in Christ Jesus our Lord.
Romans 6:23 (NIV)

What this passage speaks to is sin, whether it be a bad thought, a nasty word, an angry moment an unkind word, a lustful thought—any wrong, no matter how big or small that will be punishable by eternal death in hell. No wonder all of us have fallen short of what God requires to get into heaven! No one is good enough to get into heaven! No one! Are we, then, all going to perish in hell for eternity? We *all* have sinned!

This passage gives us the answer. The gift of God is eternal life in Christ Jesus. God knows that we cannot make it to heaven by our own doing. One little sin is enough to send us to hell forever. None of us will be good enough to get into heaven on our own. So, God gives us the most important and precious gift we can ever receive. That is the free gift of eternal life in heaven in Christ Jesus.

How do I get this free gift? What must I do to be awarded this gift of all gifts? How do I get eternal life in heaven with Jesus? The next passage from the Bible addresses those very questions:

> *That if you confess with your mouth, Jesus is Lord, and believe in your heart that God raised Him from the dead, you will be saved. For it is with your heart that you believe and are justified, and it is with your mouth that you confess and are saved.*
> *…For, Everyone who calls on the name of the Lord will be saved.*
>
> Romans 10:9-10, 13 (NIV)

All we must do to assure we will spend eternity in heaven is confess with our mouth that Jesus is Lord and was sacrificed on the cross for us and raised from the dead three days after His crucifixion and we will be saved.

But what if I've done some really bad things in my life? Maybe you have been involved in criminal activity or taken a life illegally. Perhaps you had, or are in, an adulterous affair. Maybe you have stolen from your job, cheated on your taxes, or have been divorced numerous times. Maybe you feel you have done too many horrible things in your life and there is no way God would ever listen to your prayer or want you in heaven with Him. I had those feelings when I was reading these scriptures for the first time. What does the Bible say about the feelings of hopelessness because of our wrongs?

For everyone who calls on the name of the Lord
will be saved.

Romans 10:13 (NIV)

That was such reassuring news to me. God doesn't say you *might* be saved. God says, no matter how bad you have been or how bad you are, *everyone* who calls on the name of the Lord *will* be saved!

Is it really that simple? If I believe in Christ and confess Him with my mouth, I will go to heaven? YES! Let's look at one more scripture that confirms what we have just learned. It's in the book of John in the New Testament of the Bible.

But these are written that you may believe that
Jesus is the Christ, the Son of God, and that by
believing you may have life in His name.

John 20:31 (NIV)

God assures us in this passage if we believe that Jesus is the Son of God, then we will have eternal life in heaven when we leave this life.

What is so sad is that not everyone is going to believe. There will be those who never invite Jesus into their life. They will be sentenced to eternal death in hell. Jesus gives us the freedom of choice.

How do we invite Jesus into our lives? Jesus Himself is standing on the doorstep of your soul, knocking on that door, wanting you to personally invite Him into your life. If you are feeling a tugging in your heart, I would encourage you to act upon His calling right now. There are no guarantees for tomorrow.

If you die before having asked Christ into your life, you will be destined to eternal hell. So don't hesitate. If this sounds like something you need to do, please don't wait. Right now, where you are, I encourage you to pray and personally ask Jesus to come into your life and save you. I have written out a prayer below that you can pray immediately. Please don't hesitate. All of your eternity is riding on what you are going to do *right now*! Say the words *out loud*.

If you are ready to take the most important step in your life and receive Jesus as your own personal Lord and Savior, do so by praying the prayer below:

Lord Jesus, I admit I'm a sinner and I need Your saving grace to get into heaven and to have forgiveness of my sins. I know salvation is a free gift from You. I also believe that You are God's Son and that You died on the cross for my sins and arose from the dead three days after Your death. So, Lord Jesus, the best way I know how, I personally invite You into my life right now, to be my Lord and Savior. Please cleanse me of my sins, and fill me with Your Spirit. Right now I give You my heart, mind, and soul. Thank You Jesus for coming into my heart. Thank You Jesus for saving my soul. Father, show me how to live for You. In Jesus' name I pray, Amen.

If you just prayed that prayer, congratulations! The decision you just made is the most important decision you will ever make. Your name has just been written in the Lamb's Book of Life. In other words, God has personally inscribed your name in the book of names of those people going to heaven.

I would encourage you to get involved in a good Bible-teaching church, a church that preaches about Jesus and, at the end of every service, gives those who may not know Jesus a chance to accept Him. Tell the pastor of the church you attend about the prayer you just prayed and he will help you grow and mature in your new relationship with Jesus.

If you just prayed that prayer and invited Jesus into your life, I would love to hear from you. Please write to me and tell me about the decision you made for the Lord. You may also e-mail me. Please include your name and address. Congratulations again, and God bless you!

Mark L. Franzman

P.O. Box 8358
Clearwater, Florida 33758
E-mail:
info@franzman.com

Dead But Not Buried
Order Form

Postal orders: P.O. Box 8358
Clearwater, FL 33758

Telephone orders: 727-535-4684

E-mail orders: info@franzman.com

Please send *Dead But Not Buried* to:

Name: _____

Address: _____

City: _____ State: _____

Zip: _____

Telephone: (_____) _____

Book Price: $15.00

Shipping: $3.00 for the first book and $1.00 for each additional book to cover shipping and handling within US, Canada, and Mexico. International orders add $6.00 for the first book and $2.00 for each additional book.

or contact your local bookstore